Left Behind
or
Left Befuddled

The Subtle Dangers of Popularizing the End Times

Gordon L. Isaac

LITURGICAL PRESS
Collegeville, Minnesota

www.litpress.org

1   2   3   4   5   6   7   8   9

Library of Congress Cataloging-in-Publication Data

Isaac, Gordon L.
    Left behind or left befuddled : the subtle dangers of popularizing the end times / Gordon L. Isaac.
        p.   cm.
    Includes index.
    ISBN 978-0-8146-2420-3
    1. End of the world.   2. LaHaye, Tim F. Left behind series.
3. Christianity and literature.   4. Christianity and culture.   I. Title.
BT877.I83 2008
236'.9—dc22
                                                      2008004756

Contents

Preface

A fter twelve volumes, sixty-five million copies, three movies, an endless flood of apocalyptic merchandise, four spin-off series, sequels, and prequels, the Left Behind series continues to set its own standard for publishing success. The publishing efforts of Tim LaHaye and Jerry Jenkins are impressive indeed and the impact of the most successful fiction series in human history will not go away overnight. Even though the twelve volumes are complete, it does not mean that the story is over. More books from the Left Behind point of view are being written, and the ideas they are based on continue to be set forward.

What is even more interesting is that much of the vocabulary of this mindset has entered mainstream culture. Most often people know what is being discussed when terms such as "Rapture," "Armageddon," and even such code words as "666" are employed in conversation. The other day I found myself in the express lane at the grocery store. The fellow in front of me bought a few items and the total came up to $6.66. Without missing a beat the clerk raised her eyebrows in a telling way and the fellow just behind me made some comment about the sign of the Antichrist. The Left Behind point of view cannot be escaped.

What are we to make of it all? No doubt some will extol the series as the perfect potboiler, great reading material for the beach and nothing more. Others, with heartfelt sincerity, will be grateful not only that the series has shown the applicability of the Bible to everyday life but that it has made clear the events that surround the end of the world—and all in an accessible manner! Still others have read the books and have been convinced of their need to re-order their lives in light of religious truths. Yet again, voices will be heard to say that the Left Behind series has distorted the message of Scripture and presents a form of millennial thinking that does a disservice to church and culture alike.

No matter what one's initial impression of the Left Behind series may be, it is a fact that its presence is pervasive. It is this very fact that makes further reflection on the Left Behind series a matter of great importance. What is the worldview set forward? What is the origin of this way of thinking? What is the relationship between this point of view and the relevant biblical texts? What are the theological consequences of viewing the world in this way? What are the ethical implications of end time teaching and how should one read the book of Revelation? These and other questions are worth raising and discussing in light of the publishing phenomenon that has captured the imagination of so many readers.

My own attempt to give answers to some of these questions is contained in the following pages. It is by no means exhaustive, neither is it a point by point discussion of what is found in the Left Behind books. Rather, I have attempted to ask questions that help to place the subject matter in relation to the larger world in which we live. What I have learned along the way has caused me to appreciate more fully the compelling power of the millennial mindset. In fact, that is what distinguishes this critique of the Left Behind series from others. Most other critics are content to discuss the series as a deviation from traditional biblical interpretations dealing with the second coming of Christ. While not holding back commentary on these issues, I have attempted to describe some of the social factors that come into play. When this is done, it can be seen that the Left Behind series is the product of a mindset, or perhaps better, a worldview, that is self-contained and has its own set of warrants and justifications.

As with all millennial movements, the Left Behind perspective is pessimistic about the present age and is convinced that the end of the world as we know it is right around the corner. Associated with this particular interpretation of the world is a distinctive way of reading the biblical text in light of current events. This approach to Scripture has some surprising results and helps to explain certain positions both political and theological that are taken up by proponents of the Left Behind point of view. Not surprisingly, these positions lead to very specific action in the world with a whole range of ethical implications.

As you read through *Left Behind or Left Befuddled*, you will notice that I disagree with Tim LaHaye on a number of theological points. Whatever disagreement there might be, it is not on a personal basis. It is possible to disagree theologically and still recognize each other as being fully Christian, part of a single family. Pastor LaHaye's long career of teaching and caring for people indicate his commitment to Scripture and the saving work of Jesus Christ. After listening to the video clip of LaHaye and Jenkins reflecting on the writing of the Left Behind series that can be found on the Left Behind website, it is not hard to warm to the good intentions of them both.

The six chapters of the book divide nicely into three parts of two chapters each. The first two chapters set the stage by giving an account of the size, character, and scope of the Left Behind publishing phenomenon. Chapter 1 asks the question, "What's all the fuss about and why is the series so popular?" An attempt is made to come to grips with the extraordinary size of the publishing industry surrounding the series. Chapter 2 seeks to give some background to millennial thinking generally speaking. More specifically, the historical origin of dispensationalism (the Left Behind point of view) is sketched out and traced to the present.

Chapters 3 and 4 deal with some of the doctrines central to the Left Behind point of view. Chapter 3 treats the central doctrine of the Left Behind point of view: the rapture of the church. In this treatment we find that the teaching espoused by LaHaye and Jenkins first arises in the nineteenth century, and thus is not of apostolic origin. Chapter 4 deals once again with some key biblical passages as they are taken up in the book series. Here we find that a fundamental distinction between Israel and the church drives a good deal of Left Behind theology.

The last section of the book raises questions about choices and alternatives. Chapter 5 asks pointed questions about the ethical consequences of the Left Behind point of view. The millennial mindset of Left Behind is not content to talk about prophecy but is committed to making prophecy happen. The ethical implications of this point of view are immense. Chapter 6 takes up the vexed problem of how to read the book of Revelation, the source of much prophecy teaching. One of the questions raised is, "How is the text meant to be read?" At issue is nothing less than the Christian imagination.

Whether one is Catholic or Protestant, religious or nonreligious, there is more than enough to ponder given the mainstreaming of the Left Behind point of view. These pages are offered to deepen our thinking on an important topic.

Chapter 1

What's All the Fuss About?

*L*eft Behind: *A Novel of the Earth's Last Days* was published in 1995. It is a book that is all about Bible prophecy, the Antichrist, the Battle of Armageddon and the end of the world. Few at the time it was published imagined that it would become a best seller and the center of a great deal of discussion. As a matter of fact, the original pitch for the novel almost went down in flames with the executive board at Tyndale House Publishers. Several board members doubted that anyone would buy a thriller based on the book of Revelation. Readers in the target audience were already familiar with apocalyptic readings coming out of the controversial book that comes at the end of the New Testament. When the doubters were about to squelch the deal entirely, Mark Taylor, president of the company, pounded his fist on the table and said, "If you do this right, this could sell half-a-million copies."[1] The original prediction of Taylor may have sounded high on that eventful day. But it was low, very low indeed.

Left Behind did sell the 500,000—and an additional 6.5 million copies! This is one instance in which being wrong never turned out so well. With a single title, the publishing fortunes of Tyndale House changed dramatically for the better. Overall sales tripled, catapulting a once obscure publishing house into the position of being an industry player with cash to compete for high-profile prizes. The board members who almost passed by a good thing now preside over a publishing house that is highly successful and very competitive. This newfound status has the industry leaders scrutinizing this Christian publishing house to see how they might duplicate the success of this series. "We have all watched with a certain amount of awe this extraordinary success they've had," said Barb Burg, senior vice president of publicity at Bantam Dell. "To see the numbers and the velocity at which these books have sold reminds us there's always something you can learn in publishing."[2]

In light of the great success of *Left Behind* it was an easy decision to expand the project into a twelve book series. The books have been flying off the shelves, making their way to the best-seller lists of the *New York Times,* the *Wall Street Journal*, and *USA Today*. Co-authors Tim LaHaye and Jerry Jenkins have been interviewed numerous times on shows as diverse as *Larry King Live* and the PBS *News Hour with Jim Lehrer*. A segment of a February 2003 edition of the popular television program *60 Minutes* was dedicated to exploring the trends making Left Behind so successful and to talking with LaHaye and Jenkins. It is no overstatement to say that the novels are the most successful Christian fiction series ever. The monumental success of the series is nothing short of breathtaking.

The primary writer, Jerry Jenkins, is a master storyteller whose work has won him acclaim in the publishing industry. He has authored close to twenty titles that have made their way to the best-seller list of the *New York Times*. All twelve of the Left Behind series are among them. In addition, Jenkins helped Dr. Billy Graham with his memoirs, *Just As I Am* (another *New York Times* bestseller). He has written nonfiction in the area of sports and has written pieces that have appeared in *Time, Reader's Digest, Parade, Guideposts,* and other journals. The Christian Writer's Guild, owned by Jenkins, aims to discover and encourage the next generation of Christian writers.

Tim LaHaye, whose idea it was to fictionalize an account of the Rapture, the tribulation, and the second coming of Christ, has had a long career as pastor, author, and leader within the conservative evangelical movement. He was among those who established the Moral Majority of some decades past, and more recently was named to a list of the twenty-five most influential evangelicals of the decade by _Time Magazine._ Tim and Beverly LaHaye were ranked number fifteen and labeled the "Christian power couple."[3]

A Publishing Juggernaut

A simple review of the numbers of books sold is enough to convince the most hardened skeptic that the Left Behind series is surprisingly successful. To leave it at that, however, would be to miss an important part of the storyline. There have been plenty of best-selling books that have hit the lists and disappeared just as fast as they appeared. What is singular about the Left Behind series is the nerve that it seems to have struck. The exceptionally strong sales have allowed diversification into media such as full-length movies, searchable software, a website, and spin-off series of several varieties. This added dimension has turned the series into a publishing/marketing juggernaut.

As with many best sellers, _Left Behind_ has made its way to the big screen. On January 26, 2001, the premiere of the theatrical release took place in the wake of a media blitz. Actor Kirk Cameron brought his popularity to the rendering of the journalist Buck Williams, adding his muscle to the expanding Left Behind brand. The sequel, _Left Behind II: Tribulation Force,_ was released in theaters across the country on December 31, 2002. _Left Behind III: World at War_ was released in 2005.

Logging on to the official website of the Left Behind series reveals a world of products, expanding sales lines, chat rooms, graphic novels, software innovations, further information choices, and more. As one might imagine, there are the boxed sets, calendars, greeting cards, and screensavers associated with the series itself. Available to the public are the audio books that allow one to take in one of the books in the series while commuting to and from work. In addition, a new line of dramatic audio books has been developed to bring the books to life with even greater emotion.

The *Left Behind 10th Anniversary Edition* is advertised with enthusiasm: "Now experience the book that launched the phenomenon!" Special features of this edition include a full-color, pullout timeline with Tim LaHaye's prophecy notes, behind-the-scenes commentary by Jerry Jenkins, and letters from readers whose lives have been changed by reading the Left Behind books. Just like a popular movie on DVD, this book series has added "special features" for those who want more.

The *Left Behind* novel is not only the seed for the original twelve-book series and the movies but is the inspiration for several spin-off series as well, including a military series, a political series, a graphic novel series, a kids' series, and most recently, a three-book "prequel" to the series. The military series features the same plotline as *Left Behind* but focuses on the actions of the military as the prophecies of the end times take shape. First Sergeant Samuel Adams "Goose" Gardner is on the front lines fighting against unbelievable odds as the U.S. military is swept into international intrigue. The political series features events swirling around the centers of power such as Washington, D.C. White House Chief of Staff Brad Benton is left wondering what is going on as he must protect himself against attempts on his life. All this takes place as it becomes more and more evident that his office is inexorably drawn into working for Nicholae Carpathia, the Antichrist.

The graphic novel series is an addition to a relatively new corner of the publishing industry. Graphic novels are in the style of a comic book, mostly pictures with few words, but with the sturdiness of a novel. Originally published as several comic book issues, these pictorial productions are now packaged to cover the entire plotline of the original book with more planned. Going beyond traditional comic books, the series is meant to appeal to a changing reading audience.

Another spin-off is the Left Behind series for kids. The boxed sets for kids parallel scenes from the adult series. As the website puts it, "As the world falls in around them, Judd, Vicki, Lionel, and the others must band together to find faith and fight the evil forces that threaten their lives! These books are great for kids 10–14."[4] Over ten million copies of the kids' series have already sold! One testimonial from a young reader says, "I absolutely love your books! These books are the best I've ever read, seriously. I've read all the kids books. The first time I picked up a Left Behind book I couldn't put it down. After reading those books I thought, _How can anyone read that and not believe in Jesus?_ Thanks for publishing these great books for everyone to read!"[5] Related products can be ordered, such as an age-friendly volume entitled _A Kid's Guide to Understanding the End Times_ that tells about the Rapture and how everything works out. There is also a "Kids Live Action Audio" rendering of the books that follow the adventures of the kids' series.

The Rising is the first book in a three-book series that explores the events leading up to _Left Behind._ For those who want to know more about their favorite characters, this book will reveal how Rayford's life turned him away from the family business and how he made the decision to become a pilot. It follows Buck and the others showing how their lives brought them to be "players" in the world-changing events. Further light is placed on factors at work in the life of Nicholae Carpathia, such as influential people in his life and how he came to be filled with evil.

An interesting addition to the marketing lineup is the revolutionary software known as the iLumina Edition. This software permits the user access to the complete text of the Left Behind series in Microsoft Reader and PalmReader formats. One can explore the text of Left Behind with audio and video clips, trivia questions, character profiles, and the secrets about the Left Behind series. The iLumina Edition also supplies an end times time line, and Discover Prophecy 101: an electronic course in prophecy with Tim LaHaye. Hundreds of pictures and Bible maps are available as well as a virtual tour of Jerusalem, the temple and the Tabernacle. The advertisements introduce iLumina as the world's first digitally animated Bible and Encyclopedia suite. It is touted as being a new way to read and live the Bible.

The website beckons the avid reader to sign up for the biweekly official e-newsletter of the Left Behind series. News articles, the latest concerning Jerry Jenkins and Tim LaHaye, notices regarding prophecy seminars, and other items of interest having to do with the series are offered. There are numerous ways to plug into the Left Behind community.

As if this were not enough, it is possible to subscribe to the Prophecy Club, a website and newsletter to help you understand how current events relate to the prophetic scenario set forward in the Left Behind series. As the advertisement puts it, "Each week you will get *Interpreting the Signs,* an online newsletter featuring Tim LaHaye, Jerry Jenkins, Mark Hitchcock and other end times scholars. You also have access to exclusive online message boards where you can discuss these important issues with fellow Christians."[6] It would seem that the Left Behind series doesn't end when you close the book. The surprising motive power driving the Left Behind publishing/marketing juggernaut is not merely to be read, it is to be lived! The book series may be a fictionalized account of the end times, but the truth standing behind the books demands a decision.

The website gives opportunity for seekers to become true believers in the Left Behind point of view. When one clicks on the "Live for God" button found on the homepage followed by another option that reads, "Seeking God," a message appears that states, "You've read Left Behind and you have questions. Will you be left behind?" A toll-free number is listed with the additional advice, "Talk with someone about your eternity."[7] These kinds of entries show that the Left Behind series is something more than a set of books, but a plausible scenario; an end times schemata that one can project oneself into and live out. The Left Behind novels project a millennial reality with which one can interact and in which one can live.

What's the Buzz?

There is plenty of buzz surrounding *Left Behind,* some of it positive and some of it just plain negative. One commentator with literary style in view, claims that Jenkins' writing "makes Robert Ludlum look like Shakespeare."[8] Others, unconcerned with such comparisons, avidly read the page-turners for the entertainment they offer. Advocates of the prophetic system set forward by LaHaye and Jenkins are quick to come to their defense.[9] Others are angry that LaHaye's fundamentalism has taken the book of Revelation captive.[10] The buzz surrounding the series is polarizing; either one is for it, or one is against it.

Some of the positive assessment of the series is simple and straightforward. One woman explained to me that she loves the series because the characters care for one another in admirable ways. She said, "They are really committed to each other, and they pray for each other. I wish that the Christians in my church prayed for each other like that." This woman's wishes and expectations for her own situation were realized in some small way in the undramatic portions of the book.

The entertainment component of the series is clear from sales. Many would give the books high marks because they are easy to read, have a twisting plotline, and build from one book to the next. These books may indeed set forward fundamentalist theology, but they do so in ways very familiar to popular culture, using a tried and true formula to compel the reader to buy and read the next publication. The role of the underdog in this series taps into an accepted story form which is almost universal in its appeal. The series is fully mainstream in its use of accepted forms, including that of disaster to move the story along.

Not surprisingly, the positive buzz surrounding the series is buttressed and magnified by the Left Behind website and the publishing weight of Tyndale House. The very considerable website continues the kudos and accolades that readers heap upon the authors. One can follow the activities of LaHaye and Jenkins as they offer seminars, appear at book signings, and promote the latest addition to the Left Behind family of products. Tyndale House is obliging, making room for new title offerings and encouraging a host of associated authors to join the market opening.

One such title is *These Shall Not Be Left Behind,* a work featuring the lives of real people who have been positively affected by the series. The book features over two-dozen real-life stories. In these accounts, people of various walks of life tell how they have overcome adversity through the examples presented in the books and how God has become more real to them. In the case of Jessica Cheyenne Beavers, a young woman who worked nights at a public library, the account moves from her unchurched background to reading the books to her ultimate coming to faith.[11] The positive buzz contends that the series is not just good entertainment, but something of spiritual substance and satisfaction.

The website is quite explicit in sending this message. The following short e-mail is an example of the many that have been saved in the testimonial archives on the Left Behind site:

> I myself became saved last July after several weeks of reading the Left Behind series. I had always felt that I somehow needed to get right with God, but never knew quite how to verbalize it, and the series helped me to do so! I thank God and Jesus everyday for saving me, and now daily enjoy Left Behind books, website, and e-mails. Praise God for such a wonderful way he has reached out to so many. Beau 5/17/03[12]

The books are advertised as an encouragement to readers and good tools for evangelism.

There is also negative buzz associated with the series. Loren Johns, academic dean at Associated Mennonite Biblical Seminary in Elkhart, Indiana, says that the Left Behind books "exude an evangelical warmth and passion that I find encouraging." But in spite of these positive words, his assessment is unfavorable due to the consumerist and militaristic values that are assumed in the work. In strong language he states, "I view the series as a rejection of the good news of Christ."[13] Apparently Johns is affirming the passion that the characters in the books have for Jesus Christ as the meaning of the world and as savior, but at the same time Johns is distancing himself from the specifics of the theology that informs the books.

This assessment is confirmed as Johns goes on to point out that the series is based on a misreading of the book of Revelation. The last book of the New Testament is fundamentally a revelation of Jesus Christ, not of an end time calendar. The ethical intent of the book is not just to warn of judgment but to urge believers to lives of faithful service in the world. Critical elements of Christianity such as peacemaking, stewardship of creation, and discipleship seem to be missing. "Christianity in the series," Johns said, "is cast as anti-ecumenical, materialistic and stridently pro-American, with the key characters going to Rambo-like extremes in defense of their faith." In short, Johns sees the Left Behind series as an expression of "unadulterated triumphalism" that depends on an unchristian power paradigm and destroys the Christian commitment to the way of love.

Os Guinness, a significant voice within evangelicalism and author of several books, offered his assessment of the Left Behind series saying, "It literally is junk food for the soul. And it doesn't represent the best of evangelicalism. It gives the impression that evangelicals are all irrational fundamentalists who have this apocalyptic worldview, and I think it's disastrous."[14] What is clear from Guinness' comments, given at a Christian booksellers' convention, is that evangelicalism is not monolithic in its endorsement of the theology standing behind the books. Moreover, *Left Behind* creates a worldview that Guinness cannot endorse or approve.

Surfing the web yields all kinds of comments on the series from the complementary to the very critical. Two web-based critiques show the diversity of comments and discussion surrounding our topic.[15] One labels the series, "tolerable entertainment, intolerable theology"; the other asserts that *Left Behind* is simply "bad fiction; bad faith." They both call the series into question with its wild claims and suspect implications.

Charles Henderson does so ostensibly because of the use of the doctrine of the secret rapture of the church, a development unknown in the life of the church until the nineteenth century. He wryly comments that "those of us who do not believe that events

in the early years of the third millennium are predicted and predetermined by biblical prophecy find the writings of LaHaye and
Jenkins to be more fantastic than science fiction." He goes on to
insist,

> The real strength of Christianity lies not in the offer of a miraculous
> escape from the troubles of this world, but in the inspiration to
> resist them. God offers not a last minute rescue for a few believers
> while the majority of the human race perishes in chaos, but the
> hope that was expressed so well by Jesus Christ himself in the words
> of his prayer, that God's will may be done 'on earth as it is in
> heaven.' God placed us upon this troubled planet to be its caretak-
> ers, not a frightened people who rush for the exit doors at the first
> sign of trouble.[16]

David Cloud faults the Left Behind books because they do not
present fundamentalism as they should. According to Cloud, the
series teaches a whole range of things that fall outside the Bible,
including the idea of a second chance for salvation after the Rapture, the notion that female teachers are acceptable, and the idea
that the Pope might be Christian enough to be raptured! Cloud is
in agreement with LaHaye and Jenkins in their belief in the secret
rapture of the church but thinks that it is a dangerous thing to make
fiction out of the Bible. Intermingling truth and fiction is no laugh-
ing matter, as it may have eternal consequences. Since fundamentalism is based on the notion that one must be uncompromising in
the truth, one must be willing to separate from that which is not
pure. Thus, anyone whose doctrine is not correct is considered an
outsider. According to Cloud, LaHaye and Jenkins are "compromis-
ing fundamentalists" and as such are suspect in their pronouncements. Cloud believes that the average reader of the series will be
open to misunderstanding because, from his point of view, there
is a considerable amount of false doctrine scattered across their
pages. Cloud's critique is sharp in its attack and is singular in that
it has somehow found room to be more conservative on issues than
LaHaye.

It might come as a surprise that LaHaye could be accused from the right as well as the left. That Cloud sees LaHaye's books as troubling is due in large measure because of the positive role that is given to the Roman Catholic Pope who is a saved man taken away in the Rapture. Cloud views this depiction, even though it is fiction, as ominous because it adds support to a false ecumenism and the powerful back-to-Rome movement. On this basis, Cloud gives LaHaye the pejorative title "ecumenist." An exactly opposite account is given by Gershom Gorenberg, who accuses _Left Behind_ of promulgating conservative political ideas, not the least of which is anti-ecumenism![17] Where Gorenberg sees _Left Behind_ as bashing the ecumenical movement, Cloud sees it as promoting it. These authors can't both be right, but they do depict the widely divergent opinions that have people buzzing about the Left Behind series.

Interestingly enough, Roman Catholic response to the Left Behind series has been led by two Protestant converts. Both Paul Thigpen and Carl Olsen are very well acquainted with dispensationalism and offer their respective critiques in book-length form. Paul Thigpen in _The Rapture Trap: A Catholic Response to "End Times" Fever_ argues that the doctrine of the secret rapture of the church has unbiblical origins. He asserts that dispensational interpreters have twisted Scripture in order to read this particular event into the text. Additionally, Thigpen takes some pains to show how LaHaye and Jenkins are not so subtle in their anti-Catholicism. Thigpen would have his readers understand Christianity, not from the point of view of eccentric end times teaching, but in terms of historic apostolic teaching.[18]

Carl Olsen gives his critique in _Will Catholics Be Left Behind?_ in which he gives a thorough treatment of the main theological positions of LaHaye and Jenkins. Foremost among these positions are the division of Israel and the church, biblical interpretation, and the doctrine of the Rapture.

Olsen points out that along with dispensationalism generally, _Left Behind_ portrays two distinct peoples, Israel and the church. As such there are two histories and two goals toward which God's unfolding of history moves. These purposes do not overlap. The implications of this division have huge consequences when it comes to biblical prophecy, the relationship of the Old and New Testaments, and the doctrine of the church. Olsen asserts that flawed scriptural interpretation has led to their unfortunate conclusion. According to the teaching of Christ and the apostles, "The new covenant is an establishment of a new Israel, the church fulfilling and continuing in a perfected manner the Old Testament promises and covenants."[19] Rejecting this idea, LaHaye and Jenkins undermine the importance of the church and the unifying role of Jesus Christ as the one in whom all things come together.

Olsen has much more to say about the peculiar theory of biblical interpretation that dispensationalism wields with deleterious effect. The wooden literalism at once serves to buttress the peculiar interpretations of prophecy preachers while it simultaneously serves to exclude contrary interpretations of controversial passages, thus shutting down creative discussion. As one of the main achievements of the stilted theory of interpretation, the rapture doctrine comes under careful scrutiny by Olsen. Both the rapture doctrine and the biblical interpretation by which it is established are found wanting.

Gary DeMar critiques the Left Behind series in his book, *End Time Fiction* from a reformed Protestant position.[20] In the introduction, DeMar underscores what he has in common with LaHaye. He claims that while they differ on prophecy issues, they both are squarely in the evangelical camp, affirming the reliability of the Bible and the centrality of the saving work of Jesus Christ. But beyond that, DeMar's concern is to study the theology standing behind the fictional story of the series. The question that drives DeMar's book is simply to ask, "What if LaHaye and Jenkins are wrong about biblical prophecy?" The millions who have purchased and read these books would certainly be set up for huge disappointment and reversal in the faith. His goal in writing *End Times Fiction* is to apply the theological principles of the authors to test whether or not they are consistent in applying their own method.

Negative buzz is found not only in religious but most especially in secular sources. The non-Christian world, while a little slow in acknowledging the wide popularity of the series, has also responded to the work of LaHaye and Jenkins. Citing examples of these kinds of critiques serves the purpose of coming to grips with how the book series is viewed by those who do not have common religious ground on which to stand. We would not, for example, expect these authors to affirm the reality of the return of Christ, the reality of conversion, or the necessity of judgment at the end of time.

Ann Banks in _The Washington Post_ critiques the books on three counts. The first and least weighty of her complaints has to do with style. Rather than simply stating that the books were badly written, Banks merely lets on that neither the series content nor the writing style are compelling.

More serious is the critique of the dispensational premillennial worldview and its peculiar image of God. Banks points out that the secret rapture of the church is an unusual starting point for the series. While this notion may possibly provide a decent concept for a thriller, it is quite exceptional as a belief pattern within Christianity. Banks highlights the "tortuous system of biblical exegesis" that prophecy teachers use in order to establish their particular system or worldview, all of which have consequences for the image of God that comes through in the pages of _Left Behind_.

In the second book of the series readers are introduced to a group known as "Tribulation Force," whose task is to oppose the forces of evil. The mission of this small band of believers is to fight against the Antichrist and to convert as many people as possible. Banks says:

> God softens up the populace on their behalf by raining down a succession of calamities per the Book of Revelations [_sic_], each more macabre than the last. If it's not balls of fire, it's rivers of blood (Book Four). If it's not poisoned water, it's the dimming of the sun (Book Five). And if it's not famine, it's pestilence, in the form of hideous, scorpion-like locusts, which inflict a bite so terrible that people "will want to die but won't be able to." These attention getters, we learn,

are all part of God's "master design to turn people to him so he can demonstrate his love." The Antichrist sounds sane by comparison.[21]

Banks also cringes at the depiction of the triumphant Messiah who personally vents his wrath on unbelievers by causing their eyes to dissolve in their sockets. This, she says, is one "among other video game-worthy torments." Banks goes on to say, "Plainly, this is not your turn-the-other-cheek Jesus from Sunday School. In the Left Behind series, the Prince of Peace has been recast as a rancorous bully, for whom turning the other cheek would be completely out of character."

The biting critique of the Left Behind image of God continues as Banks moves to the matter of how Jews are depicted in the series. In an act of what Banks calls "breathtaking effrontery," the authors set a mass conversion of Jews at Masada, the ancient fortress that is a symbol of Jewish defiance against Roman rule and corruption of their faith. From Banks' point of view this is not merely a matter of bad taste in placing the conversion at a Jewish holy site. Banks' secular critique has no room for conversion of the Jews at all and it would seem that conversion in principle is not welcome. Further, judgment by God at the end of time is not in her purview. While for Christian proclamation it is what makes the renewal of corrupt institutions possible, Banks seems to be offended that such a concept could be put forward in our time.

"Intolerance" is the one-word summary of Gershom Gorenberg's analysis of the Left Behind series. Intolerant political views as well as intolerant theological views drive the novels to undesirable extremes. This would not be so important if the novels were a harmless kind of entertainment. But, as Gorenberg points out, "It's fiction explicitly intended to teach." The gospel of Left Behind is one which is politically charged, showing contempt for a number of concerns and groups of people and revealing a disturbing message.

> Nor is contempt for Judaism the books' only disturbing message. They promote conspiracy theories; they demonize proponents of arms control, ecumenicalism [*sic*], abortion rights and everyone else

disliked by the Christian right; and they justify assassination as a political tool. Their anti-Jewishness is only exceeded by their anti-Catholicism. Most basically, they reject the very idea of open, democratic debate. In the world of Left Behind there exists a single truth, based on a purportedly literal reading of Scripture; anyone who disagrees with that truth is deceived or evil.[22]

Gorenberg insists that the series is intensely political. Any attempt at mitigating the views portrayed in the novels as mere entertainment does not take into account the all-encompassing paradigm that the work intends to convey.

The politics of the Left Behind series depends on conspiracy theories. A group of financiers led by the incredibly wealthy and influential Jonathan Stonegal apply pressure on the world markets to move to a single world currency. In addition, this same group pulls strings to have Nicholae Carpathia appointed the United Nations secretary-general. The Left Behind conspiracy is fictional, but it is not too far flung from some of the political views produced by the religious right. Citing the example of Pat Robertson's 1991 book *The New World Order*, in which ties between Freemasons, Jewish bankers, and Bolshevism are revealed, Gorenberg agrees with those who say that the religious right participates in the kind of apocalyptic paradigm that includes demonizing opponents and linking them with conspiracy plots of one sort or another.

In *Left Behind* the disarmament movement is led by Nicholae Carpathia in order to move toward a single global community. Every form of international cooperation, from arms control to peacekeeping forces thus becomes a tool for the Antichrist. In this way, proponents of arms control are demonized. The underlying message from LaHaye and Jenkins is that anyone engaged in these kinds of political moves is not only opposed to human freedom but is aligning himself or herself with the work of the devil. Over against this negative position, the American militia movement is cast in the role of "good guys." *Tribulation Force*, book two of the series, shows militias gathering heavy weapons as they launch a rebellion against the Antichrist. Arms control and measured work toward negotiated peace is not the political pathway to follow. The Left Behind vision of the end would have us jettison that altogether. From Gorenberg's point of view, LaHaye and Jenkins leave us with cowboy foreign policy and disengagement in world dialogue.

In the Left Behind books, bringing together the various world religions is a crucial aspect of the move to create a one-world order. Under the sponsorship of the Antichrist the leaders of the world's religions join to create the "Enigma Babylon One World Faith." Its creed asserts the basic goodness of humanity, in contrast to human sinfulness. The second highest cleric in the movement is a woman who speaks of "the great one-gender deity." The Roman Catholic Church plays an important role in this religious conspiracy as the Antichrist declares an archbishop as the global "Supreme Pope." In *Left Behind* Roman Catholicism continues to play the role of false religion that it plays in all of dispensationalism. According to this view, after the true church has been caught up in the Rapture, the false Papal Church comes into power. The scarlet-clothed woman of Revelation 17 (the whore of Babylon to use apocalyptic language) asserts herself until she is put down by the Antichrist. *Left Behind* does not depart from this oft-rehearsed script. Gorenberg sees LaHaye and Jenkins as speaking out against humanism (the creed affirming human goodness), feminism (the female cleric), and Roman Catholicism (the whore of Babylon), among other things. Religiously speaking, if you think interfaith dialogue is a good idea, you are not only wrong, but you are siding with the Antichrist.

Gorenberg considers a scene from the climax of book six, *The Assassins*, to be one of the most striking of the entire series. Rayford Steele, one of the leaders of Tribulation Force, is at an outdoor rally at which Carpathia is speaking. Rayford prays for God's guidance as he aims and fires his hi-tech handgun. The attempt appears to be a fatal shot at Carpathia. Gorenberg suggests that this is an eerie rewrite of Israeli Prime Minister Yitzak Rabin's assassination at a Tel Aviv peace rally in 1995. The disturbing factor is that LaHaye and Jenkins are on the side of the fanatical killer! Gorenberg closes this part of his critique by saying, "Having demonized religious and political opponents, LaHaye and Jenkins suggest a method for dealing with evil leaders."[23]

Gorenberg does not think that the Left Behind series is producing a right-wing conspiracy. He also understands that they do not represent the views of a monolithic religious community. Further, the book series is fiction. One could read the entire series and it may not be at the center of one's life or color one's political views. But after registering those provisos, Gorenberg is still concerned to say that the all-encompassing worldview expressed is nothing short of dangerous. In addition, the Left Behind point of view is hard to argue with precisely because it is fiction. Rather than presenting logic, it creates a mood. It creates an imaginative structure and vocabulary. It does not need to argue logically, it merely needs to leave you with a set of images, a plausible scenario to affect your thought world. Even if you don't want that particular set of structures, the creation of a thought world has been accomplished.

In the final analysis, *Left Behind* at its most basic rejects the very idea of open, democratic debate. Gorenberg quotes with approval Clark Berlet, co-author of *Right-Wing Populism in America*, when he says the religious rightists "reject the Enlightenment. For them, truth is in a book from God that has just one meaning."[24] The intolerance of the Left Behind books shows unwillingness to debate the issues. Yet, ironically enough, the fictionalized version of the end has put forth a set of proposals into the public square. Gorenberg points out that there has been a dismissal on the part of mainstream journalists and a lack of discussion of the series. Even after book six, *Assassins*, hit the bestseller list, Gorenberg says that several top staffers at a major New York publisher said they had not even heard of it. But in light of the important issues taken up by the series and the worldview set forward, Gorenberg suggests that it is time "to make the ideas woven into the fiction explicit, to analyze and rebut them." In the spirit of democratic debate, the Left Behind books must be scrutinized and discussed.

Why All the Popularity?

The Left Behind series has enjoyed unprecedented popularity. The millions of copies sold and the millions of copies yet to be sold are concrete evidence of a publishing juggernaut. It is not merely a matter of huge success; it can truly be said that the Left Behind series has set its own standard. The publishing industry has turned its head, and the boards of many publishing houses are working on ways of duplicating the great success of Tyndale House. In spite of the weighty critiques of the series, a large portion of readership continues to be convinced of the end time calendar set out. So, how does one explain the great popularity of the series? Why has it struck such a chord? Why have so many people, religious and nonreligious, become a part of the Left Behind phenomenon?

Puzzlement is produced when the question is put to those for whom dispensationalism is an unfamiliar pattern of thought. What could be so compelling about belief in a rigid sequence of events hidden by, as much as revealed in, the pages of an arcane book written in the second century? Doesn't it strain credulity to think that the book of Revelation really contains predictive prophecy for America? Wouldn't such a view require the absolute Westernization of a very Eastern text? And what of the doctrine of the Rapture? How plausible is belief in the unexpected snatching away of a portion of the population in mass confusion and hysteria? What does that have to do with the message of Scripture? The gravity-defying move may have possibilities as the opening for a sci-fi thriller, but only heaven knows where all those people will go for seven full years. How will those two-legged, made-for-earth folks fare without so much as touching foot to *terra firma* for so long? And does it really make sense to think that God will snatch away babies from their nonbelieving mothers just to complete the supposed sequence of events "souped up" by J. N. Darby and his followers in the nineteenth century?

Gorenberg, a critic of the series whom we have already met, asks with stunned concern how it is that born-again believers would identify with the heroes. They are among those who are left behind after all! True believers have already disappeared, unable to play any active role in the unfolding of the last day events. Eschatology is not the reason these books are thrillers. "The answer," Gorenberg insists, "is that in the guise of describing the last days, the books are portraying our days—but as conservative Christian readers would like them to be, without agonizing cognitive dissonance between belief and the real world."[25] Instead of working in hidden fashion, evil is open and overt as in the actions of the Antichrist. Persecution of Christians and heroism are evident and recognizable. The full number of Jews come to faith acknowledging Jesus as the Messiah. The random violence and destruction all have meaning because it is moving toward an inevitable ending foretold in Scripture.

When the question of the popularity of the series is put to the convinced, one hears a very different response. In his typically straightforward manner, LaHaye says simply that it is a "God thing."[26] He gives credit to the fact that Jerry Jenkins is a skilled fiction writer with a phenomenal ability to put into exciting format the dispensational end times calendar. He also gives credit to the fact that there is a natural interest in biblical prophecy, especially in these perilous times. Clearly LaHaye is convinced that the Rapture and the subsequent seven-year tribulation as described in the book of Revelation "has to be the greatest story in the two thousand years since Christ ascended to His Father."[27]

It is interesting that LaHaye puts it this way. No mention is made of the central teaching of Scripture, nor is there any appeal to the person of Jesus Christ, the central figure of Christian Scriptures and teaching. For LaHaye and for the dispensational approach to Christianity, prophecy is not a secondary issue but one of first importance. Viewing the text of Revelation as the source for insider information seems to take precedence over the historic teaching of the church.

In a much more pragmatic approach, Jerry Jenkins ties his comments to the market forces. When asked about the popularity of the series in an interview with Jeffery Brown, Jenkins offered that, "The sales of our books and the success of Mel Gibson's movie [*The Passion of the Christ*], I think, didn't really find a market as much as reveal a market. It didn't surprise us. We know these people are out there."[28] The Left Behind books did not create so much as tap into the ready-made market for Bible prophecy and end times scenarios. When one thinks of all the copies sold and all the individuals who have devoured each installment of the series, it is quite a market to have revealed!

These reasons cited by LaHaye and Jenkins are good as far as they go, but much more could be added to account for the popularity of the series. For example, when Jenkins says that they didn't create a new market so much as reveal one already there, the question naturally follows, "How did it get there?" Market forces which were and are in place have a history and can be described. I would suggest that there is a built-in popularity factor largely the result of the influence of dispensationalism as a movement and the specifics of earlier published works. Also, while LaHaye says that there is a natural interest in biblical prophecy in these perilous times, it may be helpful to broaden the concept slightly to embrace the fact that there is a human fascination with the end that may be even more "natural" than interest in biblical prophecy of the sort LaHaye propounds.

Additionally, it seems fair to say that the series has broad appeal because of the specific form of the writing. They are "potboilers" of a sort that have a particular American imprint. Notwithstanding that the books are sold in thirty-seven countries worldwide, there is a draw that these books have because they entertain conspiracies and insider knowledge and further because they portray the heroes as underdogs who must fight against incredible odds. Left Behind effectively uses what one might call an American plotline that translates well in today's market. Among the many reasons that could be cited for the popularity of the books these three are central: the built-in audience for the Left Behind sequence of events, the durability and adaptability of biblical apocalyptic, and the distinctively American form of the plotline.

The built-in audience for Left Behind is due to the very substantial conservative Christian denominations that hold to the dispensational point of view. Most Southern Baptists, independent

Baptists, and Pentecostals of all sorts align themselves with the LaHaye and Jenkins camp, eschatologically speaking. The numbers here are impressive indeed. If one were to take a "ballpark" census of these groups, the figures would soar into the millions of adherents. And it should be pointed out that these adherents have not remained uninformed about the intricacies of end times teaching. At present there is a dizzying array of end times teachers appearing on Christian TV, selling videos, and writing book versions of their particular type of millennial fever.

In 1971, a former tugboat captain by the name of Hal Lindsey wrote a book entitled _The Late Great Planet Earth._ As a graduate from Dallas Theological Seminary (a dispensational seminary) and a former student of John Walvoord (seminary president and dispensational author), the positions taken in his book are predictable. Theologically speaking, there is nothing new in Lindsey's book. It is no more than a popularizing of the dispensational system. In the work, however, he linked the end times calendar to current events in a manner that really took hold. During the difficult decade of the 1970s, Lindsey's portrayal of the Cold War with its possibility of a nuclear exchange, the restoration of Israel, and the imminent threat of a Russian invasion of the Middle East all served to make the book and the point of view extremely popular.

Paul Boyer, expert on millennial thought in America, thinks the significance of Hal Lindsey is that he is a transitional or breakthrough figure. His work may not have been original, but it came at a time when interest in biblical prophecy expanded beyond the borders of conservative Christianity to become a broader cultural phenomenon. People who never before showed much interest in the Bible saw how Lindsey wove together biblical passages with current events in a way that grabbed their attention and ignited the thought that there might be some credence to this kind of end time scenario.[29] Boyer asserts that interest in biblical prophecy spiked during the 1970s and has been on the rise ever since.

Lindsey's book, which was written in a very accessible style, became the all-time nonfiction book of the entire decade of the

1970s. *The Late Great Planet Earth* in both its original form and in its rewritten forms, have sold millions of copies. The work, which had first been published by a small enterprise in Michigan, was taken up by a larger publishing house. This move into a mass media marketing enterprise placed copies in airports and grocery stores, not just Christian book outlets. In other words, the appearance of *Left Behind* is not the first time publishers have realized that there is a tremendous market for prophecy books.

One also needs to take into account other books that have been prophetic precursors to the Left Behind phenomenon. One such example is the successful work of John Walvoord, *Armageddon, Oil, and the Middle East Crisis* published in 1974. And again, in 1983 the world famous evangelist Billy Graham wrote *Approaching Hoofbeats: the Four Horsemen of the Apocalypse.* The genre has been and is now very popular.

Another central reason why the books are so popular has to do with the durability and adaptability of biblical apocalyptic. Paul Boyer makes this point after a brief survey of prophecy belief over a seventeen-hundred year span of Western history.[30] In vastly different historical and political circumstances, interpreters have found vastly different meanings in the prophecies of the Bible. In the case of Revolutionary War participants, the invasion of general Burgoyne from Canada was seen as a fulfillment of Joel's prophecy. In the case of Hans Hut, one of the Anabaptists of the sixteenth century, it was clear from Scripture that Christ would return in the year 1528.

But even when apocalyptic predictions fail, the power of apocalyptic vision to shape and give energy to human endeavor is not swept away. The vision of end time events helps in the struggle to understand life, burdensome responsibilities, and one's place in history. In other words, apocalyptic is an inexhaustible source for the human interpretive enterprise. It may give emotional sustenance to disenfranchised communities seeking to challenge the established order, or it may help to support an official interpretation of political or religious significance to a recognized party.

Meanings assigned to the prophecies have not hesitated to mix political and religious themes. In our own time there has been no lack of seeing concrete political events such as the formation of the modern state of Israel as fulfilling some of the prophecies written in the Old Testament books of Daniel and Ezekiel. Interest in biblical prophecy is more than just a passing fancy. To be sure, it stands in a heightened state of interest today, but it has always played a role on some level within Western Society.

Finally, without being the last word on the series' popularity, something must be said about the American character of the plotline. One thing is clear; there is plenty of action in the books. One might not want to say that the appeal of the books is in direct proportion to the number of cars that are destroyed, but it doesn't hurt one bit that there is action aplenty throughout the twelve books. Colliding cars here, the occasional bomb there, sprinkled liberally with conspiracies of various sorts and some disasters taken directly from the book of Revelation as though they are to occur quite literally, and you have the motive power for the series. Yes, the story does lead up to the battle of Armageddon and the glorious appearing of Jesus, but it is really the action and not the theology that keeps things moving. It doesn't hurt that the heroes use the latest technology like satellite phones; it makes the books have an up-to-date feel to them.

Beyond the clear appeal that the series has in using fast-paced action, one cannot overlook the appeal of insider information. As one who is let in early on the secret of end times events, the millennial believer is aware of where the plot leads, while others are not. Nicholae Carpathia, the suave Rumanian who turns out to be the Antichrist, may fool some, but for those who know, his identification is merely a matter of putting the pieces together. Indeed, everything has meaning and everything fits. If you are someone who reads the Bible as a coded script, it is very important to know that the end times have started. In that new scenario which begins with the Rapture, religious and civic actions must change to suit the times. In this frame of reference the world is a novel in which every detail has meaning and only those who are initiated "get it."

Rod Dreher tells of his anxiety at age thirteen when events in the world looked very ominous.[31] American hostages were in Tehran, the Soviets were in Afghanistan, and he had become fixated on the fear of nuclear war. However, once he was introduced to dispensational premillennial teaching the chaos all made sense; there was no need to be afraid, for it was all a part of God's plan. Once inside the belief structure, buttressed as it is with insider information, interpreting the world takes particular shape. The Rosetta Stone helps to chart a course through what are by anyone's standards unusually anxious and difficult days. Dreher says that it is easy to see why so many people want to believe in a way out of the trouble.

Charles Henderson has as good an answer as anyone when he says that the novels are as "American as apple pie." Likening them to the old grade "B" cowboy movies, he insists that "They traffic in the currency of one of the most powerful American myths: that of the hero who rescues the damsel in distress."[32] The prospect of being saved in the nick of time alleviates the need for a lot of unnecessary worry. As long as one can read the signs of the times, the offer of riding off into the sunset unscathed by the tribulation is yours for the asking. In *Left Behind* the ultimate escape from the world of woe is framed as a grand rescue to a realm beyond. In the classic American myth the sunset serves to shield from us the marital spats that hero and the heroine must have in real life. In *Left Behind* the sunset is heaven that assures that we do not have to deal with the world as it really is.

As we reflect on Left Behind as a book series and as a phenomenon one thing is clear: it has its proponents and its detractors. The very nature of the apocalyptic vision presented in the series leaves one either on the outside or the inside. If one is a proponent of dispensational premillennialism, one is on the side of the good. If one does not share that position, one is relegated to the group of scoffers and those who will most likely be left behind. This kind of fundamentalism is a polarizing form of thought that has its own set of justifications. Exploring the history and construction of this point of view is the topic for the next chapter.

Chapter 2

The Rise of Dispensationalism

The Left Behind series is nothing if not a system of understanding biblical prophecy from a particular vantage point. The very clear sequence of events starting with the rapture of the faithful and proceeding to the seven-year tribulation, the emergence of the Antichrist, the conversion of many unbelievers, the battle of Armageddon, and finally the glorious appearing of Jesus, stands opposed to any other way of understanding the fulfillment of time, including other Christian ways of understanding end time events. Only those who agree with dispensational premillennialism share the truths of the Left Behind perspective. Tim LaHaye, while recognizing that other sincere believers down through the centuries have identified their own times with the culmination of all things, is convinced that humanity is only now in a position to claim with certainty that we are in the end times. He claims that more signs of Christ's return exist today than at any time in history. Detailing the scenario has been the subject of his many books.

To gain insight on why this might be the case, we turn now to some historical background. In order to be able to place and evaluate the Left Behind perspective, it will be important to know something of the nature of apocalyptic thinking generally speaking and more specifically, Christian apocalyptic thinking. If we take the story of the rise of dispensationalism within the context of the broader use of biblical prophecy, it will also give us a platform from which to analyze some of its distinctive features. What we will find is that the Left Behind point of view has a special home within the American religious scene with its cultural peculiarities and affinity for voluntarism.

Modern readers who are only familiar with the latest speculations regarding how America fits into biblical prophecies may be surprised to learn that expectation of a marvelous consummation has had a long history not exclusive to the Bible. In the face of the instability and uncertainty of life there exists an unshakable belief in the idea that all things will eventually be made right. At the consummation, the forces of evil will be overcome and laid to rest; the agents of evil will be confronted, brought to justice, and rendered harmless; and the elect will gather in idyllic community on an earth made new.

Early Prophecy Belief

Norman Cohn traces the ancient roots of this apocalyptic faith by looking at the belief patterns of Egyptians, Mesopotamians, Vedic Indians and Zoroastrians. He maintains that until about 1500 BC a diverse number of peoples all agreed that in the beginning the world had been organized and set in motion by gods or a god. The good of the known world is revealed through victory in war, fertile land, and stable social relations as encoded in custom and law. Where these goods remained, the security of the people went unchallenged. However, that order was never untroubled; it was always threatened by evil destructive forces whether natural—floods, plagues, famine, or other disasters—or whether man-made—wars, or tyrannical conquerors. This conflict between good and evil, otherwise known as the combat myth, was given various formulations. A young god or hero was given the task of keeping the forces of chaos at bay; in return he was made the ruler of the world.

According to Cohn, sometime between 1500 and 1200 BC Zoroaster broke with this static formulation in favor of one that suggested that there would be a final resolution to the anxious tension of the combat myth. A time would come when a momentous battle would take place in which the supreme god and his supernatural hosts would defeat the forces of evil and their human allies and eliminate them once and for all. As Cohn tells the story, this new and radical reinterpretation of the combat myth influenced Jewish communities, especially that of Qumran, and through that association affected Christian thinking on apocalyptic topics.[1]

If we turn to early Christian thinking about the final consummation, we find an interesting and varied approach. To reduce the matter to its simplest terms, there were three groups: 1) Christians who believed in a messianic kingdom that would last a thousand years before the final consummation, 2) Christians who did not acknowledge this, and 3) Gnostics who passed under the name of Christian who were also nonmillennialists. The difference between these groups, among other things, had to do with the role of resurrection in their thinking and the interpretation of a brief passage in the book of Revelation.

The millennium, of keen apocalyptic expectations, is mentioned only once in Scripture. The passage in question reads as follows:

> Then I saw an angel coming down from heaven, holding in his hand the key of the bottomless pit and a great chain. And he seized the dragon, that ancient serpent, who is the Devil and Satan, and bound him for a thousand years, and threw him into the pit, and shut it and sealed it over him, that he should deceive the nations no more, till the thousand years were ended. After that he must be loosed for a little while. (Rev 20:1-3)

Many Christians interpreted this passage as a predictive description of the drama to take place at the end of time. For them, the millennium was regarded as quite literal. This literal reading of the text extended over the subsequent passage and included two separate resurrections.

Estevao Bettencourt offers a helpful summary of the millennial position in Christian theology:

i) the second coming of Christ, in majesty; ii) the first resurrection, that of the just only; iii) a general judgment, of the nations as a whole, not of individuals; iv) a messianic kingdom lasting a thousand years; v) the second resurrection, that of all men; vi) last judgment, of all persons individually; vii) the eternal destiny, reward or punishment.[2]

This form of millennialism, or chialism, seems to have been in the ascendancy in the early Christian era.

Yet, there were other Christians who did not read Revelation 20 in a literal manner, remaining instead with a more straightforward explanation of the consummation. In this view the second coming of Christ marks the end of the age. At that time the dead will be awakened from their sleep. In the words of Jesus, "Do not marvel at this; for the hour is coming when all who are in the tombs will hear his voice and come forth, those who have done good, to the resurrection of life, and those who have done evil, to the resurrection of judgment" (John 5:28-29). This utterance of Jesus seems to indicate that resurrection, judgment, and reward take place without the intervention of a thousand years. Calculations or specific end time prophecies do not seem to play a role in his accounting—only the coming of the Lord. Thus, many early Christians did not follow the elaborate millennial position described above.

Irenaeus of Lyons, an early proponent of millennialism, lived in difficult days. He witnessed a terrible persecution of Christians in Gaul around AD 177. As if this were not enough, there was also the considerable threat of heretical teachers such as Marcion, Basilides, and the Valentinians. While there are subtle differences among these heretical theories, they held in common the belief that there is a God above the God of creation. Since matter was deemed to be evil, salvation was conceived as release from bodily existence and escape from the earth altogether. At death the "inner man" was said to ascend directly to eternal blessedness in the realm of untrammeled purity. Christian discussion of the resurrection of the body struck these thinkers as quite appalling. It could only be considered as returning to the impurity of matter. Given this theological position, there could be no celebration of the resurrection of Jesus and the beauty of a redeemed creation. They disdained such notions as describing the opposite of salvation and the mere resuscitation of the body into a nightmarish zombie-like entrapment in the flesh.

Against the Gnostic assertion that the creation was unredeemable, Irenaeus courageously set out the doctrine of the goodness of creation at the beginning of time, and the hope of redeemed creation at the end of time, including the resurrection of the body. In a similar fashion, Justin Martyr, also a second-century Christian apologist, protested against the heretics passing as Christians saying, "some who are called Christians . . . who say there is no resurrection of the dead, and that their souls, when they die, are taken to heaven." He calls such people "godless, impious heretics" and warns his readers not to be deceived by them: "Do not imagine that they are Christians." In contrast, he insists, "I and others, who are right-minded Christians on all points, are assured that there will be a resurrection of the dead."[3]

In a second line of argument, Irenaeus speaks to the issue of the intermediate state addressing Gnostic and Christian alike. From what we can tell of the sources, both groups were nonmillennialists maintaining that the soul departed on high at death. If this were true, Irenaeus countered, it must have been true for Jesus as well—but such was not the case. For three days "he dwelt in the place where the dead were" and ascended to the Father only after he had risen in the flesh. No disciple is above his master, and none of the redeemed will ascend to the Father without first entering into Hades, the place of death.

Charles Hill maintains that there seems to be a connection between the two doctrines of the millennium and the intermediate state. The heretical dualists as well as the nonmillennial orthodox affirm that one enters into the full presence of God upon death. This belief, at least on a systematic level, renders an earthly kingdom beside the point. Irenaeus, who holds the opposite view, takes pains to teach that there remain two things before one is ready to enter into God's presence: the sleep of death in Sheol (Old Testament) or Hades (New

Testament) just as Jesus had experienced it, and then the resurrection of the just and the millennial kingdom. For Irenaeus, the millennium serves the function of allowing the righteous to grow, becoming accustomed to apprehending the glory of God.[4]

One important lesson that emerges from this early stratum of Christian teaching is that there are two distinct streams of thought. The one is millennial in its orientation, reading the remarks of Revelation 20 in a more or less literal fashion, linking a subterranean intermediate state with a millennial hope. The other is nonmillennial in its orientation, reading the remarks of Revelation 20 in a more or less nonliteral fashion, and usually opting for a heavenly intermediate state without a literal earthly millennium. These two traditions exist within Christianity down through the ages. At one period of history one moves into the ascendancy, while at times the other gains momentum.

Prophecy in Medieval Times

The story of the medieval church is how the nonmillennialists, or amillennialists came into the ascendancy. Key in this important shift was Origen (ca. AD 185–254) who attacked millennialists for misreading apocalyptic texts whose meaning should be taken figuratively. He complained that they were given to a carnal form of thinking and that they were too lazy to use their heads. As Christianity gained recognition and standing in society, especially after Constantine came to power in AD 312, the millennialist strand faded. The fading of millennialism may have been due as much to the withdrawal of direct persecution as much as the arguments of authors such as Origen, but there were important voices speaking out on the subject.

St. Augustine (354–430) added his considerable weight to the matter with the writing of his *City of God*. In this influential work the metaphor of history as the struggle between two cities is set forward. The heavenly citizenship of Jerusalem is pitted against the earthly or fleshly citizenship of Babylon. In the end, the two cities will finally and forever be separated. The essential point of Augustine's teaching was to assert that the eschatological drama was being played out in the here and now. The interpenetration of temporal and eternal is such that God alone can sort things out. In the interim one must remain vigilant and align oneself with the city of God.

Augustine's viewpoint eschews speculation regarding an end time calendar. It is not particularly futuristic in its appeal. Rather, the coming of Christ lends meaning to all of life. Literalist readings were cut off and ideas of an earthly millennium receded into the background. At the Council of Ephesus in AD 431, millennialism was condemned and Augustine's views prevailed. Ironically, Augustine's perspective ruled supreme for approximately a millennium.

Prophecy During the Reformation and Beyond

At the time of the Reformation, wholesale change at every level of society struck with catastrophic force. As social structures threatened to collapse, apocalyptic fervor fanned the flames. Predictions of Christ's return multiplied. The Peasants' War, with its huge numbers of slain, left a pall over the German territories.[5] And when Jan Matthys, an Anabaptist leader, gained power in an important city in Westphalia, things went from bad to worse. The city was declared to be the New Jerusalem and many of its prominent citizens were forced to leave. It was declared that all property would be held in common.

Matthys died in an ill-advised attack against the besieging forces, and was succeeded by Jan Bockelson (John von Leyden), a twenty-five-year-old tailor. The dire circumstances of the city pressed the inhabitants on two fronts. From without, the siege effectively cut supplies threatening imminent starvation; from within, Leyden's authoritarian rule terrorized the population. Polygamy was forcibly instituted, and anyone who objected was summarily executed. Even though John von Leyden took upon himself the title of Messiah, it could not save him from the seizing of the city, his capture, humiliation, and final execution.

Europe looked on in horror, denouncing and fearing the apocalyptic actions of the Anabaptists as much because of the threat of insurrection as the brutality that followed in John von Leyden's path. The removal of government and the apparent loss of all restraint challenged one of medieval society's most highly coveted values: regulated authority.

Martin Luther (1483–1546) agreed with the negative assessment of this Anabaptist attempt to bring in the kingdom of God through direct action and force of arms. The private revelations of ecstatic leaders were regarded by him at best as human delusions or at worst as demonic deceptions. However, Luther's rejection of the enthusiasts did not keep him from using the text of Revelation to understand the turbulent world in which he found himself. Luther was convinced that the end of all things was not far off. This realization did not come by way of a speculative end time calendar. Luther was convinced that the preaching of the Gospel provokes the anger of the devil and thus brings us closer to the final advent, but it also creates space for a time of grace before the coming day of the Lord.

Luther saw himself not so much as a Reformer as a preacher sent by God to bring the Gospel to light in his own time. As such, the apocalyptic structure of Luther's thought is shown as he preaches the liberating word of the Gospel. He considers it his God-given work to point out the blasphemy of the devil, to expose his surreptitious mode of operation, and to rail against Satan (Hebrew), Diabolus (Greek), or the Detractor (Latin). Luther's defiance of the devil is at once the practice of exposing sin for what it is and simultaneously a bold pronouncement of the truth of God.

Luther's approach to biblical prophecy allows that such matters as the little horn, the man of sin, the Antichrist, the beast, and the Babylonian harlot of Revelation 17 all apply to the developing history of Christianity and to the ongoing struggle between Jesus Christ and Satan within the Christian Church, culminating at the end of time. Some, but not all, of the events subsequent to the first century believers can be traced in the early chapters of the book.

Later chapters are yet to be fulfilled. This became known as historicism, or a historicist reading of the book of Revelation.

In direct opposition to this view, the futurist view emerged. It was natural that Jesuit scholars who were sworn to protect and uphold the papacy found different ways of reading the texts. The Spanish Jesuit Francesco Ribera (1537–1591) projected the Antichrist into the future (thus the term "futurism"). Ribera applied the Antichrist prophecies to a future personal antichrist who would appear in the end time and continue in power for three and a half years. In essence, Ribera said, "Antichrist prophecies have nothing to do with the history of papal Rome, rather they apply to only one sinister man who comes at the end." In this way the reputation of the pope was rehabilitated. For nearly three centuries futurism was largely confined to the Roman Catholic Church. But in 1826 Samuel R. Maitland (1792–1866), librarian to the Archbishop of Canterbury, published a pamphlet promoting Ribera's ideas. It is no small irony to think that a majority of conservative Protestant Christians, who have significant differences with Rome, would take over this approach first developed by Ribera.

Prophecy in America before the Civil War

At the time of the founding of the Colonies, many in England were unsatisfied with the progress of religious change in that island country. The chance to begin anew was attempted with a profound sense of God's overruling providence. America was a land of opportunity not primarily in an economic sense, but most particularly in a religious sense. This was an unprecedented chance to begin anew, a chance to get it right. Where England had failed to constitute a true commonwealth under God, the new colonies now had their chance.

John Winthrop (1588–1649) in the famous speech given on the deck of the _Arbella_ before the colonists disembarked in the new world, made clear the divine context of their undertaking. "When God gives a speciall commission he lookes to have it stricktly observed in every Article." Having entered into covenant with God, Winthrop reminds his fellow colonists of the urgency of complying with the stipulations, otherwise "The Lord will surely breake out in wrathe against us." The work they have set their hands to is the divine work summarized by the prophet Micah, "to doe Justly, to love mercy, and walke humbly with our God." To that end, the colony is to supply the needs and necessities of others, to deal with others in "meekness, gentleness, patience and liberallity." The work is undertaken not privately but as a part of God's providential plan. "For wee must Consider that wee shall be as a Citty upon a Hill, the eies of all people are upon us."[6] The colonists may have been establishing a new commonwealth in a new country, but it was as the new Israel in which prophecy played a key role.

The American colonial period is marked by attempts to understand itself with respect to God's plan. As in Winthrop's vision, America is seen as the new Israel, a fulfillment of God's plan to reveal his goodness to the nations. The idea that God had designed this continent to be an asylum of freedom is promoted later in the history of the country by Lyman Beecher.[7] Sounding clearly among the leaders of the day was the millennial vision consisting of a transformed society.

Against this backdrop of Christian confidence and an optimistic reading of history, the account of the Millerite movement makes for an interesting contrast. Contrary to the reforming zeal of the voluntary societies and the crusaders for social causes, William Miller (1782–1849) led a movement of a different kind. His Second Advent doctrine was based on a pessimistic view of society. He was convinced by his reading of Scripture, most especially the prophetic passages, that the incremental purifications achievable through social reform movements would not be enough to attain the goal of the millennial age. Only divine intervention of the most dramatic kind would be able to bring that about. It was this message of warning of the "Advent near" that animated William Miller and caused him to dedicate his life to "arouse a slumbering world to duty."

William Miller was born in Pittsfield, Massachusetts. He acquired a common school education and spent considerable time reading to improve himself. While farming had been his major occupation in his early years, later he was promoted to the office of sergeant in the militia, and called to fill the civil offices of constable, sheriff, and justice of the peace. He received a commission in the army and served in the War of 1812. At this time many of his friends were skeptics and deists under the influence of the writings of Voltaire, Hume, Payne, and others. Miller too found himself conflicted over the matter of religion. As he put it:

> While I was a Deist, I believed in a God, but I could not, as I thought, believe the _Bible_ was the _word of God_. The many contradictions, and inconsistencies, which I thought could be shown, made me suppose it to be a work of designing men, whose object was to enslave the mind of man; operate on their hopes and fears, with a view to aggrandize themselves.[8]

As Miller thought about Christianity he "viewed it as a system of _craft_, rather than of _truth_."

However, all this was to change. Miller's thoughts had turned again and again to eternal questions of life, death, and judgment without resolve. Finally, on a Sunday in mid-September Miller was called upon to read a written sermon in the absence of the pastor. As he stood in the pulpit beginning to read the sermon, he found himself overcome with emotion. The skepticism of his deist leanings and the words of faith contained in the sermon wrestled over his conflicted soul. He sat down weeping, unable to finish. As Miller was later to describe it, "At length, when brought almost to despair, God by his Holy Spirit opened my eyes. I saw Jesus as my friend, and my only help, and the word of God as the _perfect rule_ of duty."[9]

Some of Miller's skeptical friends attempted to overthrow his conversion through some of the arguments he had formerly used against the Bible. This was a challenge that the analytical mind of William Miller took up with urgency. He was convinced that if the

Bible were a revelation from God to man that it had to be consistent with itself, its parts must harmonize, and it must have been given for instruction and therefore for human understanding. With these thoughts in mind, Miller set out to deal decisively with the apparent contradictions in Scripture. This led to several years of intense Bible study and rumination on Scripture.

In the wake of Miller's devoted study he developed fourteen rules for interpreting Scripture. A close reading of the rules reveals that the rationalism that at one time was used as an excuse for unbelief was now turned to a reasoned ordering of everything in the Bible, including prophecies. As Miller says, "to understand doctrine, bring all the Scriptures together on the subject you wish to know; then let every word have its proper influence, and if you can form your theory without a contradiction, you cannot be in error."[10] Noncontradiction is a means for substantiating one's reading of a topic. The human expositor could efface himself and offer up his interpretations—not as human speculation—but as deductions from the Bible, the source of all divine knowledge.

When seen in this light, the Bible is not a book of mysteries but a record that is eminently reasonable. It is proved true by the unity of expression from Genesis to Revelation. Further, the facts of recorded history, when measured against the fulfillments already recognized, show the reliability of the sacred text. William Miller described his own experience in the following quotation:

> I laid by all commentaries, former view and prepossessions, and determined to read and try to understand for myself. I then began the reading of the Bible in a methodical manner; and by comparing Scripture with Scripture, and taking notice of the manner of prophesying, and how it was fulfilled, (so much as had received its accomplishment,) I found that prophecy had been literally fulfilled, after understanding the figures and metaphors by which God had more clearly illustrated the subjects conveyed in said prophecies. I found, on a close and careful examination of the Scriptures, that God had explained all the figures and metaphors in the Bible, or had given us rules for their explanation. And in so doing, I found, to my joy,

and as I trust with everlasting gratitude to God, that the Bible contained a system of revealed truths, so clearly and simply given that the "wayfaring man though a fool need not err therein."[11]

Reading the Bible convinced Miller of the fundamental truths of sin and salvation that form the central narrative of Scripture, but there is more. Miller also became struck with the fact that "God had in his word revealed _times_ and _seasons_," that "the end of all things was clearly and emphatically predicted, both as to time and manner." As the gravity of this thought began to work on his mind it became evident that William Miller had a moral obligation and duty to deliver this special message to "a dying and perishing world."[12]

Miller preached salvation in Christ alone, but to that he added his premillennial beliefs as well. Briefly put, Christ will come in glory with his saints and angels. At that time the dead saints will be raised, the bodies of those living will be changed, and all will be caught up in the air (1 Thess 4) to be judged and presented to the Father. During this time the earth will be cleansed by fire according to the words of 2 Peter 3:10. Satan and the wicked dead are shut up in the place reserved for the damned. The saints will reign with Christ on an earth made new for one thousand years. Then the wicked dead will be raised, the devil set loose, and war waged. The judgment will vindicate the righteous who then possess the earth forever. As Miller put it: "I understand that the judgment day will be a thousand years long. The righteous are raised and judged in the commencement of that day, the wicked in the end of that day."[13]

J. N. Darby and Dispensationalism

John Nelson Darby (1800–1882) was born into a distinguished Anglo-Irish family. John was named after the famous Admiral Horatio Nelson with whom his uncle Henry had served in the Royal Navy. Darby had a distinguished career at Trinity College Dublin and served briefly as a lawyer before his conversion. Thinking that it would be more suitable for him to serve in the church, he was ordained deacon in 1825 and in the following year became priest.

After he became convinced that the hierarchical church was corrupt and entirely ruined, he joined the Brethren movement with its anti-institutional bias. There Darby made his home, eventually ascending to a position of being one of their most gifted teachers.

Darby operates with a fundamental dichotomy that shapes all of his thinking. According to him, God has two completely different economies of operation, one for an earthly people (Israel), and another for a heavenly people (the church). "Prophecy applies itself properly to the earth; its object is not heaven. It was about things that were to happen on the earth; and not seeing this has misled the Church."[14] The church has gone wrong by thinking that the many prophecies all but bursting from the pages of the Bible apply to its own future, when in point of fact they do not. "The Church is something altogether apart—a kind of heavenly economy, during the rejection of the earthly people, who are put aside on account of their sins."[15] His system of vindicating future events is the solution to the problem that is the beginning point for his theology.

The system that Darby effectively promoted in his several trips to the United States is based on the belief that God's plan for his earthly people has been revealed in a series of covenants. In each successive age or dispensation, God stipulates a law or regulation that serves as a test for human responsibility. The characteristic of each dispensation is the failure of mankind in fulfilling the requirement and the resulting judgment of God. Darby envisaged a total of seven covenants or dispensations. As one covenant gives way to the next God continues to care for his earthly people, but because of their constant failure they have to endure the domination and oppression from the Gentiles.

The dispensationalist reading places great emphasis on the seventy weeks that are spoken of in the prophecy of Daniel 9. During the opening seven weeks, the city of Jerusalem is rebuilt. After an additional sixty-two weeks the Messiah is to come and the prediction of his rejection ("an anointed one shall be cut off") is fulfilled. This leaves only the actions contained in the last week yet to be completed. It is in this week that war and desolations appear. Darby is certain that the Antichrist is referred to when the passage mentions "the prince who is to come." Abominations occur until the appointed end is made of the Desolator.

In order to avoid the problems of date setting that had plagued the Millerite movement, and to give a more flexible reading of the seventy weeks in Daniel, a "postponement theory" was devised. In effect, it was asserted that the last week of Daniel's prophecy was suspended. This was due to the fact that the Jews rejected Jesus as the Messiah. In light of this fact, Christ postponed his scheduled return and unexpectedly turned his attention to the Gentiles. As a result, God set to work building up a new people, a heavenly people— the church. The postponement theory places the Christian church in a hiatus or prophetic time warp.

But this creates yet another problem: when does the prophetic clock start ticking again, and how will God proceed with his final plans for Israel? It is precisely at this juncture that dispensationalism has posited its most controversial and distinctive doctrine—the secret pretribulational rapture of the church. The doctrine asserts that Christians will be mysteriously and precipitously taken from the world, leaving unbelieving Gentiles and Jews behind. Its importance centers on the fact that this move marks the resumption of the prophetic calendar, removes believers so that they will not have to endure the great tribulation, and inaugurates the events concluding God's direct work with the Jewish nation.

The reason this is controversial and distinctive is that up until the 1830s all reference to St. Paul's words about being caught up in the clouds (1 Thess 4), for those Christians who read the words literally, were understood as an action tied to the second coming of Christ. In J. N. Darby's teaching the catching away of the saints was separated from Christ's appearing. The Rapture thus becomes the first in a two-stage coming of Christ. The Rapture is secret in that no one sees the Lord, who is visible only at the great appearing. Familiar to most dispensationalists is the succinct formula: at the Rapture, Christ comes _for_ his saints, and at the Second Coming he will come _with_ his saints. Between these two events the last prophetic week unfolds with the great tribulation, the revealing of the Antichrist, and all the other events on the dispensationalist calendar. In this way Darby was able to solve the problems created by the newly formed system of thought.

While the exact doctrinal origin of the secret rapture may be shrouded with some degree of uncertainty, there can be no doubt that the presuppositions of Darby demanded its existence. Once a thoroughgoing distinction between Israel and the church had been accepted by him, reading the doctrine in the pages of Scripture seemed simple and clear.

> It is this conviction, that the Church is properly heavenly in its calling and relationship with Christ, forming no part of the course of events of the earth, which makes its rapture so simple and clear; and on the other hand, it shows how the denial of its Rapture brings down the Church to an earthly position, and destroys its whole spiritual character and position. Prophecy does not relate to heaven. The Christian's hope is not a prophetic subject at all.[16]

Only when the church is lifted out of the earthly sphere can the prophetic clock begin ticking again.

According to Darby, once the "Marriage of the Lamb" (the secret rapture) takes place, then the divine script for the final chapter of earth's history can unfold. Shortly after the rapture of the church, the Antichrist is revealed. Offering peace in a time of world chaos, he makes a covenant with the newly restored nation of Israel, offering to protect it from hostile neighbors. In an act of treachery, the Antichrist cuts off the renewed religious practices of the Jewish people and demands to be worshiped as God. All opposition, even that of Jews who have come to newfound faith since the Rapture, is ruthlessly suppressed. In direct response to the harsh treatment of his own people, God pours out terrible plagues on earth. The suffering of creation and the people of earth can only be described as the great tribulation.

As pressure mounts to a zenith, forces from north, south, east, and west will converge on Israel in a vast attempt to destroy God's people. The armies depicted in the prophecy of Ezekiel will gather in a valley of northern Israel for the world's ultimate battle, Armageddon. Just as it looks as though the forces of evil will win the day, the glorious Christ with the raptured saints will break through the clouds and destroy the enemies of God.

As the seventieth week of Daniel comes to an end, the Antichrist and his host will be thrown living into the lake of fire. Satan will be bound and thrown into the bottomless pit. Christ will set up the millennial rule in Jerusalem where the promises of God given to the Jewish people unfulfilled during the time of the first advent will be completed during Christ's second advent. At the end of the thousand years, Satan will be released to foment one last ill-fated rebellion. Once this is put down, the resurrection of the dead and the final judgment take place. Everyone who has ever lived is assigned a place in either heaven or hell. God then proceeds to create a new heaven and a new earth reserved for his peoples, the new earth given to the Jewish people and heaven reserved for the church.

This two-storied system called premillennial dispensationalism gained followers starting from the first trips of J. N. Darby to the United States. The small group of believers grew steadily to become a movement. The real boost to the acceptance of the system came through at least four important impulses: a set of strategic biblical prophecy meetings known as the Niagara Bible Conferences, the Scofield Reference Bible, the Modernist–Fundamentalist Controversy, and the earth-shattering shock of the First World War.

Enthusiasm for teaching on biblical prophecy and issues related to the second coming of Christ was running high among the laity and the clergy in the years just after the Civil War. The time was right for advocates of premillennialism of both the dispensational and the more historic type to seize the offensive. To this end, the first International Prophecy Conference was convened in New York City in 1878. James H. Brookes, Presbyterian minister of enormous influence in the beginnings of dispensationalism, acted as the chairman of the self-constituted committee in charge of the conference. The conference was constituted as an interdenominational gathering which was typical of much Protestant work of the time. This gave the meeting the possibility of cross-pollination; and in this case, the views of the dispensational type could and did receive a hearing within a broader evangelical constituency, thus bolstering dispensational standing within conservative Protestantism.

New York City was selected as the site for the conference in which the premillennial return of Jesus Christ was stressed. The common cause of organizers and attendees was to bring to light the doctrine of the personal return of Christ, a teaching that many were constrained to believe had long lain in neglect and disregard. A stand against postmillennialism (the belief that Christ would return after the gradual betterment of society) became a point of unity, even though significant differences stood between the historic and dispensational approaches to the premillennial return of Christ. At the end of the conference certain truths were affirmed, including the absolute authority of Scripture, the literal interpretation of Old and New Testament prophecies, the imminent and personal return of Jesus Christ, the progress of evil in this present day, and the duty of the church to watch, pray, and work.[17]

The Scofield Notes to the Bible are the second factor that supported and solidified the growth of dispensational thought. C. I. Scofield is a figure about whom not a lot is known. His past is reported to contain several shady episodes including the desertion of his wife and two daughters and being ousted from the position of state district attorney on account of unethical financial dealings.[18] But in spite of what might be said of his character, Scofield's importance for the movement is unquestionable. Ernest Sandeen insists that, "in the calendar of Fundamentalist saints no name is better known or more revered."[19]

Scofield was befriended by James H. Brookes and participated in the Niagara Conferences, being asked to lead studies from time to time. In 1888 he wrote his first work entitled, *Rightly Dividing the Word of Truth*. This piece contains the hermeneutical principles which both reveal and reassert the presuppositions of dispensational thought. Scofield asserts that anyone who would "rightly divide"

Scripture must reckon with and differentiate between three categories of people: Jews, Gentiles, and the church. This highly controversial starting point for interpreting Scripture assures the divisions that characterize dispensationalism, and continue to exert their influence up to the present.

Even more important for the telling of our story is the place held by the Scofield Reference Bible. First published in 1909, the dispensational point of view was set forward with illustrative comments and cross references printed with the text of Scripture. The work was very popular, selling two million copies by 1945 and another million between 1967 and 1979.[20] The numbers alone reveal the pervasive influence of Scofield's interpretation. But additionally, for generations of conservative Christians this way of viewing things "is just the way it is." As Ernest Sandeen puts it, "The book has thus been subtly but powerfully influential in spreading those views among hundreds of thousands who have regularly read that Bible and who often have been unaware of the distinction between the ancient text and the Scofield interpretation."[21] Many Bible Schools, institutes, and seminaries claimed this form of dispensationalism as their own, promoting it to almost confessional status.

The third factor that promoted dispensationalism was the Modernist–Fundamentalist Controversy. Mid-nineteenth century events set the stage for a polarization in the religious world, led by the publication of several scientific and literary studies. The radical shift in the intellectual climate can be seen in the development of new theories related to geology, biology and literary and historical criticism. The new geology set aside Bishop Ussher's calculations of the earth's age, based as they were on a strict reading of the Bible. The new scientific approach made it possible for Charles Lyell (1797–1875) to rewrite the Genesis account of the origin and early history of the earth. But it was the new biology as set out in *Origin of the Species* (1859) by Charles Darwin, that was to symbolize the new intellectual climate. The idea of evolution was not entirely new, having been put forward by G. W. F. Hegel (1770–1831), Comte (1798–1857), and Herbert Spencer (1820–1903). In fact it was

Spencer, not Darwin, who showed the full significance of thinking in an evolutionary fashion in a series of books. Applying the theory to biology, sociology, psychology, and ethics meant that a new way of looking at the world emerged, which fostered a philosophy of development so critical to the modern era. This was also to have its effect even in the area of biblical studies. The influences of Darwin's theory seemed to many of the time to be antithetical to Christian belief and thus "atheistic." At all events the new theories and their application bolstered the growing "higher criticism" of the Bible.

There were two reactions to this state of affairs: the Modernists attempted to receive the new discoveries and incorporate it into their view of the Christian faith, while the fundamentalists tended to be much more suspicious of the new learning and to hold out for the old truths. But the issues were certainly present from the middle of the century onward, and religious sentiment tended to be increasingly polarized in the swirling changes of the late century.

The earth-shattering shock of the First World War is the fourth factor that aided the rise of premillennial thought in America. Modernists had downplayed the supernaturalist worldview, affirming instead trust in cultural development. The kingdom of God is thus reflected in the reform and betterment of society. Western Christian Civilization in both its European and its American forms seemed the best hope for the world. But with the onset of a world war, the overly optimistic view of liberal Christianity was discredited and the pessimistic worldview of premillennialism seemed to fit the times more accurately.

Before World War I most premillennialists had stayed aloof from cultural concerns, but once the cultural element was added everything changed. The collection of theological ideas referred to as premillennialism became the "fundamentalist" movement. It was now clear that the differences between the Modernists and the fundamentalists were not merely a debate about theology. The watershed of the First World War made clear that the differences included nothing less than the whole moral course of civilization.

As George Marsden points out, "This position accentuated the longstanding paradox in the thinking of American premillennialists. As premillennialists they had to say that there was no hope for culture, but at the same time they were traditional American evangelicals who urged a return to Christian principles as the only cultural hope."[22]

As Timothy Weber puts it, "No event in the fifty years after 1875 did more for the morale of American premillennialists than World War I."[23] The conflagration on the European continent and the moral decline in American society and religion gave powerful confirmation of their dire predictions about the inevitable corruption of the age. This occasioned a careful searching of Scripture for the significance of the world war for biblical prophecy. The emerging fundamentalist movement flexed its muscle at two well-attended conferences in Philadelphia and New York where questions concerning the war were discussed. The increased hearing for dispensational views raised confidence in the movement. "Though times were tragic, things were never better for American premillennialists."[24]

Dispensationalism from WWII to the Present

Premillennial prophecy watchers saw World War I as proof of the declension of culture and the quickening pace of developments as outlined in their belief pattern. But if the barbed wire and the trenches of France could lead to the singular conclusion that the end is near, how much more would the firebombing and the concentration camps of World War II underline the dark and pessimistic views of dispensationalism? The human and social loss associated with World War I was sobering and tragic, but the devastation of Hiroshima was nothing short of staggering to the imagination. How could anyone speak of the new atomic era into which mankind had stepped except to use apocalyptic language of the most lurid kind? If World War I released dispensationalism from its oppressed minority status, then World War II legitimized and promoted it as nothing had before.

Hiroshima and Nagasaki provided new rich territory for prophetic speculation. Biblical texts were read and reread to see if atomic weapons were mentioned in Scripture. Many were drawn to the passage in 2 Peter that speaks of the day of the Lord saying, "The heavens will pass away with a loud noise, and the elements will be dissolved with fire, and the earth and the works that are upon it will be burned up" (1 Pet 3:10). Wilbur Smith, well-known prophecy teacher and professor at the newly formed Fuller Theological Seminary, published a pamphlet entitled "This Atomic Age and the Word of God" that sold over fifty thousand copies. In it he showed how the atom bomb had changed our world forever and how it fit into the sovereign work of God.

Never before in history had such destructive power been seen. The fear aroused by the prospect of atomic annihilation produced divergent responses; activist scientists petitioned those in government for an atomic energy control plan, but prophecy teachers like Smith used the opportunity to refer others to the wisdom of the Bible.

> For years, Bible students who have dared to speak of the Biblical teaching that this age will end in a catastrophe have been laughed at, called all kinds of names—literalists, fanatics, chiliasts, medievalists, etc., etc. Now the atomic bomb seems to be persuading some who delighted in ridiculing those who had earnestly tried to interpret the eschatological portions of the Word of God in a sober way, to recognize that this earth may be nigh to a disaster, a final disaster more terrible than was ever depicted by any modern student of prophecy.[25]

Wilbur Smith, at least by his own accounting, was one of the more circumspect prophecy teachers who did not indulge in wild speculation. Nevertheless, his exposition of 2 Peter relates the Greek text and applies it to particle theory and what was known in the day regarding atomic energy. Although he disavows that Peter was predicting the atomic bomb, he does assert that "the principle involved in nuclear fission, which is at the base of the atomic bomb, is the principle which Peter here sets forth."[26] Explaining prophecy in the latest terms and up-to-date style is something of the stock-in-trade for teachers and writers in the genre. Wilbur Smith did this as well as any.

If World War II brought with it the atomic bomb, it also saw the emergence of Russia as a new world power. Older accounts of the Ottoman Turks as the "Gog" mentioned in the book of Ezekiel gave way to musings over the place of Russia in biblical prophecy. Russia first became the object of some speculation in this regard early in the nineteenth century. With the beginning of the Crimean War (1853–1856), which pitted Russia against England, the identification of Gog with Russia became more and more accepted in prophecy circles.

The third and most important development since World War II is the founding of the State of Israel in 1948. In contrast to historic premillennialists like William Miller, who said that a reestablishment of an earthly Jewish state would have no prophetic significance whatsoever, dispensational premillennialists with their hermeneutic of special consideration in Jewish interests saw in the establishment of the Jewish state a fulfillment of prophecy and yet another sign of the imminence of the return of the Lord. When the Jewish National Council proclaimed Israel a nation on May 14, 1948, many hailed the action as the greatest piece of prophetic news of the twentieth century. For dispensationalists, the founding of the nation of Israel meant that Jesus could come at any moment.

The Six-Day War of 1967 also plays heavily in the calculations of dispensationalist teachers. For the first time since Babylonian captivity, Jerusalem came into the hands of the Jews. This is important not only because Jerusalem is the traditional capital of Israel but also because it includes the temple compound. For dispensationalists, who believe that the temple will eventually be rebuilt and sacrifices reinstituted, it was exhilarating to see the temple site come into Israeli hands.

The fourth theme played out in prophecy teaching after World War II has to do with the role the United States must play. If Russia is Gog and the United States is the other superpower, then it stands to reason that the United States must perform some countervailing role. As logical a statement as this may seem, it must be reiterated that according to dispensational thought, the United States does not play as special a role in prophecy fulfillment as Israel does. Dispensationalism is deeply skeptical of *all* human structures and governments. Many prophecy teachers hold out a bleak picture of the United States, especially when it comes to moral issues. Dispensationalism is particularly sensitized to the materialism and secularism that is inundating Western culture with the inevitable outcome of God's judgment.

Portraits of modern America by prophecy teachers are most often bleak, comparing our society with warnings found in Scripture. They are quite pessimistic about America and continually point out that perilous days lie ahead. Prophecy writers were and are unfailing in their critique of common culture with its disregard for biblical morality. Warnings of moral collapse may engender discussions of a wide array of deficiencies including the breakdown of the educational system, decadent popular music with its corrosive effects, the rising tide of sexual immorality, abortion, and conspiracies of various kinds. Declension and apostasy are watchwords of the prophetical teachers.

The fifth theme is the role of the Antichrist and the demonic order ahead. Wilbur M. Smith may have been reticent to claim that Mussolini was the personification of the Antichrist, but he was not retiring when it came to speaking about what he saw as the central threat to freedom in our time. He was of the conviction that the atomic bomb and the call for atomic energy control was leading inevitably to a single world government. This kind of internationalism would mean the loss of national sovereignty, the introduction of a world police state, a world education which would be nothing more than brainwashing, and a world religion which would substitute the spirit of world citizenship for true faith.[27]

The Characteristics of Dispensationalism

After this brief historical review of the rise of dispensationalism, the markers and methods that LaHaye uses in the Left Behind series look surprisingly familiar. Against this history it can be seen that the work of LaHaye and Jenkins is not really something original but something that falls into line with the movement that started in the nineteenth century. The rise of dispensationalism has a history like any other that when studied reveals growth and development as well as characteristics that define the movement: its belief pattern, its ethos, and the manner in which it argues its case. It will serve us well to set out a few of them for the sake of analyzing the movement.

For Tim LaHaye, as well as for all of dispensationalism, prophecy is the major theme of the Bible. This is the doctrinal assertion of past leaders in the movement and it is clearly the position of LaHaye. One only needs to peruse the list of publications by LaHaye to prove this out. Of the approximately forty-four books that he has authored, a majority are on the topic of prophecy.

As the story of the rise of dispensationalism shows, early in its development the doctrine of last things functioned as a buttress against unbelieving skeptics. The ability to point to specific prophecies that had been fulfilled in history was proof that stood against the corrosive comments of the higher critics. Biblical prophecy was thus a key to establish a bulwark in support of the authority of the Bible. It was and is the _terra firma_ of dispensational teaching and precisely so is to be found at the center of their particular Christian expression. Simultaneously, prophecy promotes evangelism among the unbelieving. Dispensationalism has always taken seriously the command to go into all the world to make disciples of all nations. Urging hearers to get ready for the imminent return of the Lord is a natural way to fulfill the command of Christ. But equally important is the manner in which this action functions sociologically within the movement.

The preaching of biblical prophecy establishes a world of discourse that creates its own cadence and audience expectation. It is meant to inform through insider knowledge brought by way of ancient biblical prophecies and their application to life in today's uncertain world. This is knowledge that cannot be obtained by merely looking at the facts as they stand around us but can only be acquired through divine interpretation. Interestingly enough, by use of the so-called "literal" interpretation, the interpretational range is already selected to make sense for the average layperson willing to be led. If the interpretation is called "literal," it sounds to any democratically experienced audience like it should be eminently reasonable and achievable by everyone. Prophecy facts help to lock believers in a particular community of discourse that marks itself out from others.

The belief pattern of dispensationalism is also heavily dependent on the anti-ecclesial foundations laid by J.N. Darby. The empirical church is to be held in suspicion. The role of believers, therefore, is seen in isolation from the "institutionalized church." Since the mainline Protestant denominations as well as the Roman Catholic Church sojourn in apostasy, dispensationalism sees its role as the remnant that preserves the faith. Seen within the context of the decline of civilization, it is no wonder that the notion of the church existing as a kind of guerilla resistance movement awaiting the army of liberation makes sense in this system of thought. *Tribulation Force* (book two in the series) embodies this exactly as it depicts the struggles of a small band of believers during the period of great tribulation.

Additional distinctive beliefs include the total separation between Israel and the church, the secret rapture of the church, the doctrine of the Lord's imminent return, all of which mark a clear departure from traditional Christianity. Dispensationalism as a form of fundamentalism has a distinct profile well-suited to the American landscape. It may well be problematic for those outside looking in, but it is a complete system that has its own set of warrants and justifications for those who make their home within the movement. Taking a closer look at those justifications and warrants will be the topic of the next chapters.

Chapter 3

The Secret Rapture of the Church

The opening pages of *Left Behind* follow the progress of a flight from O'Hare to London Heathrow. Rayford Steele, the pilot of the full 747, enjoys the first hints of the sun as it dispels the blackness of the sky with pastels of a gentle dawn. As the plane approaches the scheduled 6 a.m. landing all seems well until one of his flight attendants informs him that "People are missing." It is only the emotional state of the otherwise cool and composed co-worker and the pandemonium that soon erupts throughout the plane that convinces Rayford that something unusual is afoot.

Investigating for himself, the evidence soon mounts. Just scanning the seats nearly causes Rayford to panic. There is no way to account for the number of empty seats. Against everything that his scientific mindset can offer for explanation, he must wrestle with the fact that the impossible is upon him. As he looks closer he realizes that the missing passengers' shoes, their socks, their clothes, everything is left behind! Seatmates cry out, screaming and leaping from their places. Calming the passengers is out of the question, just trying to keep the hysteria at a low roar is all the crew can hope to accomplish. Radio contact with the outside world yields no explanation.

Rayford pleads ignorance with his crew in the midst of the screaming, pain, and disbelief. The chaos is overwhelming, but not

51

so much that Rayford cannot recall the conversation he had with his wife Irene before his departure. In that exchange his overly religious wife had made mention of the rapture of the church. She had been reading everything she could get her hands on about that subject. Whether he liked it or not, Irene had informed him of her belief in a happening of monumental proportions. When the events on the plane become clear, Rayford realizes that Irene had been right. He, and most of the passengers, have been left behind.

The effects on the ground are depicted with even more frighteningly gruesome detail. The consequences of the Rapture leave cars and eighteen-wheelers careening unmanned. The collisions, snarled traffic, and crumpled wreckage have left the world in a condition worse than a mere crisis. Every level of government, every utility company and civil function, has been touched by worldwide devastation. Essential services are interrupted, people are stranded at airports and train stations. In the middle of carrying out simple daily tasks people disappear right before the eyes of others who are left behind. A groom disappears while putting the ring on his bride's finger. A nurse reading a monitor at the delivery of a baby suddenly vanishes, her uniform, stockings and all, ends up in a pile on her empty shoes.

The children play a large role in the tragedy surrounding the Rapture. The movie account of *Left Behind* shows a woman emerging with bloody head from a car accident wandering aimlessly crying, "My baby, my baby, where is my baby?" In the book an account is given of a father who captures on video the disappearance of his baby as it is in the process of being delivered![1] From what we are told, all children under the age of ten, whether in a Christian family or not, are taken in the Rapture. The catastrophic effect of this action alone can hardly be put into words. The Rapture is not a quiet event that leaves things as usual; the Rapture alters all action on earth ever after.

A quick word about terminology is in order. I speak of the *secret* rapture of the church to indicate the unique position of dispensationalism on this point. The Left Behind point of view insists that there are those who are taken out of the world before the revelation of Jesus Christ and judgment. To speak of Christ coming near to the earth without revealing himself as Lord is to speak of an invisible, sudden, or secret coming of Christ. This is singular in the history of Christian teaching. Tim LaHaye objects to this terminology, preferring to speak of the *sudden* rapture of the church.[2] But whatever terminology is used, the issue is that the Left Behind point of view separates the second coming of Christ into two stages: one in which the returning Christ does not reveal himself, and the other in which he does.

How one takes the description of the rapture of the church as set out in *Left Behind* depends on your point of view. One cynical blogger points out that the Rapture as a starting point for a science fiction thriller is a pretty good concept. He says it in the following irreverent manner: "There are a couple of exciting scenes in the novel—no, wait, let's be exact here. There are precisely two exciting scenes in the novel. The first is at the beginning. The second is at the end. In between is a vast wasteland of repetitive, pointless action and unconvincing spiritual conquests."[3] The blogger, admittedly without any Christian sympathies, views the Rapture scene only in terms of its utility as a writing tool—as a starting point for a fiction plot. It ranks right up there with the scene at the end of the book in which Nicholae Carpathia blows away two individuals in broad daylight and gets away with it.

For those convinced of the reality of the Rapture, the opening of the book reveals the role that the Rapture plays in charting an end times calendar. The final words of the first chapter find Rayford Steele, an unbeliever, admitting the reality and the truth of the Rapture. Irene, his religious wife, was right. Earlier in the chapter Irene's musings had been simply but effectively expressed to the effect, "Can you imagine Jesus coming back to get us before we die?" This simple statement of the matter hides several problematic aspects of the teaching, but it does reveal what the authors of *Left Behind* take for granted, namely, that the Rapture is a teaching that comes directly from the Bible. As the character Irene states, "I only believe what the Bible says."

Irene's character clings to an apparently commonsense stance. What possible objection could be leveled at believing what the Bible says? What is not so readily apparent is that this is a verbal marker of a very particular kind for the Left Behind point of view. As we have seen in an earlier chapter, dispensational doctrine is based on three nonnegotiable pillars or thought forms: literalism with respect to biblical interpretation; the parenthesis theory; and the dichotomy between Old Testament Israel and the New Testament church. What Irene urges on behalf of all Left Behind adherents is a literalism when rendering biblical language. Literalism is the hidden key that determines who is within and who is outside a valid approach to Bible prophecy.

The secret rapture of the church is only one expression of a commitment to this so-called literal hermeneutic. Several other instances of literalism—that appear to be at the heart of the Left Behind scenario—also serve to buttress an unflagging commitment to a "biblical approach" to the end times. For example, Tim LaHaye believes that there will be cataclysmic topographical changes predicted in the Bible. The Mount of Olives, we are told, will be split in two to form a valley running east and west. This is to become the valley in which the final battle of Armageddon is to take place. Again, Mount Zion will be elevated above the surrounding hills and the rest of Palestine will be transformed from a mountainous terrain to a great fertile plain. And finally there is to be an earthly as well as a heavenly Jerusalem that is to exist. The heavenly Jerusalem is to float above the earth and is to have a foundation 1500 miles square and is to be 1500 miles high!

Anyone who does not believe what Irene does apparently does not have a simple belief in what the Bible says. The verbal markers are quite clear, if one does not agree with the Left Behind point of view one is playing fast and loose with Scripture and is a part of that apostasy that LaHaye and Jenkins are fighting against. But is this the only or the best way of viewing the witness of Scripture? In what follows, we will take a look at biblical considerations touching on the doctrine of the rapture of the church. A close reading of the critical texts reveals a presentation of the Second Coming that does not affirm the Left Behind point of view. Next, some scrutiny of the system of biblical interpretation used by LaHaye and Jenkins will be undertaken. There we will find that the commitment to a so-called literal hermeneutic causes LaHaye and Jenkins to press Scripture into a particular mold. And finally a word or two needs to be said about what a vision of the redeemed future might look like without the doctrine that so dominates the Left Behind system of thought.

Biblical Considerations

As pointed out by Hitchcock and Ice, "The Left Behind Theology is built upon a belief in the Rapture."[4] The Rapture teaching that is so important for the Left Behind series is based on the idea that the second coming of Christ consists of two stages. The first stage is characterized by Christ coming secretly near the earth (the parousia), at which time all true believers will be caught up in the air with him and taken away to heaven, while those whose Christianity was false, pagans, and Jews who have not received Jesus as Messiah, will undergo a period of intense suffering called the tribulation. Or, to put it in other words, Christ returns twice: first, *for his church*, which will be spared the great tribulation (the Rapture); then later in power and glory *with his church* to conquer his enemies (the glorious appearing).

An official Left Behind site on the Internet declares: "In one chaotic moment, millions of people around the world suddenly disappear leaving their clothes, wedding rings, eye glasses and shoes in crumpled piles. Mass confusion hits while vehicles suddenly unmanned veer out of control, fires erupt, and hysteria breaks out as the living stare in disbelief and fear at the empty places where their loved ones were just seconds before. This is the Rapture that God has planned as the first sign to begin the unraveling of the end of time."[5]

Is this what the Bible teaches? There are several reasons to dispute Left Behind's teaching regarding the secret rapture. In the first instance, when one turns to 1 Thessalonians 4, which gives an account of the coming of the Lord, it is not at all secret but seems to depict a full manifestation of Jesus Christ in his power and glory. The passage does not spell out a rapture only meant for the church but the personal and visible return of the risen Christ. The Scripture says:

> But we would not have you ignorant, brethren, concerning those who are asleep, that you may not grieve as others do who have no hope. For since we believe that Jesus died and rose again, even so, through Jesus, God will bring with him those who have fallen asleep. For this we declare to you by the word of the Lord, that we who are alive, who are left until the coming of the Lord, shall not precede those who have fallen asleep. For the Lord himself will descend from heaven with a cry of command, with the archangel's call, and with the sound of the trumpet of God. And the dead in Christ will rise first; then we who are alive, who are left, shall be caught up together with them in the clouds to meet the Lord in the air; and so we shall always be with the Lord. Therefore comfort one another with these words. (1 Thess 4:13-18)

Tim LaHaye writes that the Rapture "is taught clearly in 1 Thessalonians 4:13-18, where the apostle provides us with most of the available details."[6] But when one considers the text in its natural reading, one finds none of the details imported into it by LaHaye. There is no indication that there will be a twofold coming of the Lord in this text. The reference is quite simply to "the coming of the Lord." The church for almost two millennia has taken this passage to refer to the second coming of Jesus in which he will reveal himself to all humanity, not a snatching away of the church. It is no wonder then that there is also no mention of the "tribulation" which is a factor critical to LaHaye. To posit that the great tribulation must intervene between the Rapture and the glorious appearing of the Lord (book twelve of the series) is mere supposition that cannot be predicated upon the text. Further, while the text does say that believers alive at the return of the Lord will meet him in the air, it does not say that they will be housed in heaven for seven years during the time of tribulation only to emerge from this intercalation to resume participation in the end time calendar of dispensational imagination. This view can only be achieved through the worst sort of special pleading.

If Paul is not setting forward a rapture of the church what is the point of this passage? In the first instance we must see that the context of these comments is grief. The Christians of Thessaloniki are grieving the loss of some of their number. Paul's concern is to give a word of comfort—not speculation—to the believers confronting the harsh reality of death, and to do so he turns to the death and resurrection of Jesus. The apostle is teaching the ones in his care how to grieve in a Christian manner as opposed to the desperate and excessive mourning that typified pagan funerals. From Paul's instruction it is reasonable to assume that the Thessalonians thought that the living had an advantage over the dead when it came to coming into the presence of the Lord. Most often, we in our time assume just the opposite. But against both of these assumptions Paul goes back to the Resurrection as he thinks through this problem. Everything hangs on what happened to Jesus—his death and resurrection. Even as God the Father vindicated the Son and raised him up out of death through bodily resurrection, so too, the believer's hope is centered in Jesus' resurrection. The logic of the argument is clear as it is simple; through Jesus those who have fallen asleep and those who remain alive will be brought through all obstacles, including death, to be in the presence of the Lord. Paul does not seem to be interested in giving an end times calendar for people to follow. His exposition is a bit of Christ-centered teaching that emphasizes the Resurrection, not a disembodied interlude in a midair holding pattern.

What kind of language is Paul going to use when referring to the age to come? By the very nature of the case adequate language and images are going to be hard to come by. I like the way that N. T. Wright puts the problem when he asks, "How do you describe the color blue to a blind person? If someone has never been able to see, how can you even convey the idea of color, let alone the difference between colors?"[7] That is the problem that we as Christians face whenever we talk about the world that God intends to make one day—when Jesus appears and puts all things right.

Wright goes on to explain that it might be possible to "translate" the language of color into something else, say, taste or sound of one sort or another. One might say that red is a hard and bright color a little like blaring brass, and green, on the other hand, is a restful or calm color, more like the tone of a woodwind instrument. Of course these kinds of analogies are hopelessly inadequate to the task, but they give some idea of the differences between red and green to someone who would like to know but does not have the facility to experience it in the present. Using an array of mental pictures painted through the help of metaphors is one way of getting an idea across to an intended audience, in this case a blind person.

The difficult problem that Paul must deal with is how to describe a singular event that is to take place in the future! What language does he use? In this passage he paints a verbal picture of the descent of the Lord out of heaven accompanied by various dramatic signs. Paul does not use this verbal picture exclusively. In 1 Corinthians 15 he uses the language of the transformation of the body, in Philippians 3 he uses the language of the salvation that comes to us from across the sea, and in Colossians 3 he speaks simply of Jesus appearing. In our passage Paul chooses to use the language of descending and ascending and in so doing evokes several images familiar to his audience.

The first is the Sinai picture where Moses has been in the presence of the Lord. He alone enters into the cloud of God's glory that covers the mountain where he receives and comes down the mountain with the Torah. The descending Moses is met by the elders of Israel who have ascended the mountain to meet him. Paul's listeners may well have had in mind the number of ways in which Jesus is the new Moses of the people of God.[8] But what is central in the Sinai picture is the way in which the ascending and descending takes place. It is not that Moses and the elders go up the mountain to stay but that they come down to ground level in order to live out the commands of God.

The second is the picture of Daniel 7 and the vision of the vindication of the people of God. Daniel depicts war on earth of epic proportions and the people of God suffering. One "like a son of man" (7:11) representing those who are oppressed ascends to the Ancient of Days with the clouds of heaven. There judgment is rendered on behalf of "the saints of the Most High" (7:22). They are vindicated, that is, released from the suffering they have been experiencing, and given possession of the kingdom. This courtroom setting is one in which the suffering people of God are lifted up, rescued from the oppressors, exonerated, and established in the presence of the Lord.

When we turn to 1 Thessalonians 4 we see that the allusion to Daniel 7 works in a similar manner. The Thessalonians are in the role of the son of man in his sufferings. Jesus takes the role of the Ancient of Days and we are going up on the clouds to meet him. The action moves toward the vindication of the suffering Thessalonians, even those who have "fallen asleep." Paul uses the vision of the vindication of the people of God as found in Daniel and applies it to the circumstances of his own day. The suffering Thessalonians are lifted up, rescued from the oppressors, exonerated, and established in the presence of the Lord.

It must be noted here that the application of the Daniel 7 imagery in the first century had nothing to do with concrete up and down movement. The vision of Daniel is not so much a literal rendering of time and space activity as it is the verbal rendering of what the prophet has seen going on in God's realm. The activity taking place on earth can only be given proper evaluation as one views it in relation to what is happening in God's sphere of activity. In the perspective of the biblical world, heaven and earth are not two hermetically sealed compartments that have no interface. Rather, there is a complex relationship between the two that is revealed in the actions of God as he rules through the Word.

The third layer of metaphor that Paul uses in painting the picture in 1 Thessalonians 4 comes from the first-century customs surrounding rank, royalty, and honor-giving. In the event that an illustrious visitor, or even the emperor himself, was to visit a colony or city, expectations had to be filled. As the emperor approached, a delegation consisting of important personages would go out from the city to meet the monarch. The delegation would thus join the retinue and proceed to escort the emperor back into the city. To do so was simply to show the honor due the visitor. It may well be that the honor given to Jesus at his triumphal entry reflected this custom (Matt 21:1-17).

That Paul's picture was understood in this way is shown by the following excerpt from a homily given by the famous St. John of Chrysostom (ca. 347–407). In his exposition of 1 Thessalonians, John asks, "If Christ is about to descend why will we be caught up?" The answer he gives is simply, "To show him honor."

> For when a King drives into a city, those who are in honor go out to meet him; but the condemned await the judge within. And upon the coming of an affectionate father, his children indeed, and those who are worthy to be his children, are taken out in a chariot, that they may see and kiss him; but those of the domestics who have offended remain within. We are carried upon the chariot of our Father. For He received Him up in the clouds, and "we shall be caught up in the clouds" (Acts 1:9). Seest thou how great is the honor? and as he descends, we go forth to meet him, and, what is more blessed than all, So we shall be with him.[9]

Clearly for St. John Chrysostom the "catching up" event Paul describes in 1 Thessalonians 4 parallels the custom of giving honor to an illustrious visitor. Going outside the city to meet the visitor does not imply that the retinue will stay outside the city. The aim is not to stay where they meet but to come back to where judgment and celebration is to take place. The scene depicted is part of the culmination of the end of the age, when Christ shall return as the ruler of the cosmos. There is nothing secret about this return; it is open for all to see and will reveal the final vindication of God's people and will bestow the honor due to the One risen from the dead.

Now that we come to this point certain conclusions can be made, both negative and positive. Negatively, this passage does not support the kind of freight that LaHaye and other dispensationalists import into it. In this portion of his advice to the Thessalonians, Paul is not sketching out a schematic for an elaborate end times calendar. He is not engaging in speculation but consolation. There is no mention of tribulation, saints living in heavenly homes for seven years to return for the millennium, or any other set of calculated events. Central in this passage is a discussion of resurrection and how Christians, who used to be pagans, should think about these things. Further, to read the passage in the manner of LaHaye and Jenkins demands that one interpret away "the voice of the archangel" and "the loud command" and the overriding fact that the passage is speaking about *the coming of the Lord.* To interpret this account as indicating a secret rapture of the church where the coming of the Lord is not really the revealing of the Lord is odd in the extreme. It means, contrary to the text, one has to presuppose a secret coming of Christ and then read Scripture in light of that prior belief. This is an unusual sort of literal interpretation indeed.

On the positive side of the ledger, several comments can be made. The language of Paul in his letter to the Thessalonians, while simple, evokes a range of images and allusions that help to place his comments in the context of the grand narrative of salvation. It is no advantage, Paul asserts, if you are living at the time of the Lord's return. The dead will not be blocked from the benefits of the kingdom any more than the living will have an undue priority over those who are asleep at his coming. The passage focuses on the goal toward which God's saving plan is moving—the gathering of God's people together and the kind of proclamation that is thereby warranted. The apostle ends this passage with the admonition, "Therefore, comfort one another with these words." The proclamation that comes out of this New Testament passage is the centrality of Christ and his saving activity, the certainty of the coming of the Lord and the ensuing resurrection, not a pretribulation rapture of the church.

Another key passage in sorting out the Rapture doctrine is 1 Corinthians 15:51-57. In this passage the apostle Paul is talking about the fact that God will remake heaven and earth and will redeem humanity in the midst of that mighty act of creation. At issue is the difficult problem of how this mortal and decaying body can be changed into the new transformed physical nature of the resurrection. In 1 Corinthians 15 Paul uses different imagery than that of 1 Thessalonians. Instead of a circumstance where he must deal with the question of grief, Paul is compelled to speak to those who are convinced that there is no resurrection of the dead (1 Cor 15:11), opting instead for certain Hellenistic notions of salvation that imply escape from the body and escape from the earth. Against these notions we find Paul asserting the goodness and redeemability of God's creation. Here he presents the reality and beauty of resurrection, and he does so using the language of transformation.

> Lo! I tell you a mystery. We shall not all sleep, but we shall all be changed, in a moment, in the twinkling of an eye, at the last trumpet. For the trumpet will sound, and the dead will be raised imperishable, and we shall be changed. For this perishable nature [body] must put on the imperishable, and this mortal nature [body] must put on immortality. When the perishable puts on the imperishable, and the mortal puts on immortality, then shall come to pass the saying that is written:
>
> "Death is swallowed up in victory."
> "O death, where is your victory?
> O death, where is your sting?"
>
> The sting of death is sin, and the power of sin is the law. But thanks be to God, who gives us the victory through our Lord Jesus Christ. (1 Cor 15:51-57)

The discussion at the end of the book of 1 Corinthians deals with the end of all things. It has that in common with the Thessalonians passage. But while the Thessalonians passage uses the ascent and descent imagery of Christ's coming, this passage from 1 Corinthians 15 uses the language of being "changed in a moment, in a twinkling of an eye." Both texts speak about the same event—the coming of the Lord and the end of all things—but do so using different terminology because of their relative audiences. The apostle Paul must shape his arguments to the various churches with their particular concerns. In both passages Paul asserts that the living and the dead will have equal treatment and that all the people of God will participate in a general resurrection that accompanies God's judgment of the world.

This passage mentions, as with the Thessalonians account, "the last trumpet." This image is associated with the end of the world, the vindication of the righteous, and the judgment of the world. In other words, it is verbal imagery that signals to any reader familiar with the tradition that we are dealing with apocalyptic matters. We are not dealing with the penultimate, as in "a sign to begin the unraveling of the end time." What we have is the event itself. For *Left Behind* to interpret this account as something less than the final coming of the Lord requires one to close one's ears to the loud command and the sound of the trumpet—to misinterpret what the apostle is saying.

A scene approximately halfway through *Left Behind* shows Rayford Steele playing a prerecorded tape made by pastor Vernon Billings, a fictional character in the initial book of the series. As the pastor believed that he would be taken away in the Rapture, he had the foresight of preparing a video tape to instruct those left behind. Following his description of the sequence of events is quite revealing. Purporting to follow the argument of 1 Corinthians 15, Pastor Billings explains, "When these things have happened, when the Christians who have already died and those that are still living receive their immortal bodies, the rapture of the church will have taken place."[10] 1 Corinthians 15 does indeed speak of the transformation from perishable to imperishable. The resurrection is squarely in view in the passage in question. What one cannot find, however, is any reference to the rapture of the church. It simply does not occur in the text, neither is it implied. Pastor Billings' words are nothing more than pure speculation. It is as though the idea were pulled out of thin air. 1 Corinthians 15 says nothing about anyone being left behind and nothing about a pretribulation rapture.

The sequence of events as described by Paul is rather straightforward. First comes Christ's resurrection. As Paul says, "But each in his own order: Christ the first fruits" (v. 23). Second comes the resurrection of believers at the Second Coming, "then at his coming those who belong to Christ" (v. 23). After these events the consummation takes place, "Then comes the end, when he delivers the kingdom to God the Father after destroying every rule and every authority and power" (v. 24). In the account of the apostle Paul there is no elucidation of an intervening seven-year period and no mention of two comings of Christ. If the apostle Paul was trying to set forward the doctrine of the rapture of the church, he made a rather bad job of things.

Two additional items embedded in the fictional videotape deserve a quick mention. Speaking of the raptured, Billings makes this confession: "I believe that all such people were literally taken from the earth, leaving everything material behind."[11] This is a singular assertion in light of the biblical impulse that makes a great deal of holding the spiritual and the physical together! Salvation is not the escape from the material but precisely its redemption. God's creation of human and animal life is a celebration of the material; it is neither something to regret nor is it a problem to overcome. The Rapture doctrine shows itself to be perilously close to the Hellenistic conception of salvation that disdains created reality. While paying lip service to resurrection, LaHaye would have us believe that once granted resurrection life, believers immediately enter into a nonmaterial existence for seven years. Rather than corroborating the biblical affirmation of the resurrection of the body, it would seem that the Rapture doctrine actually undermines it.

Second, in what could be considered a "throw away" line, pastor Billings continues describing the rapture of the church by saying, "He has removed his church from a corrupt world that seeks its own way, its own pleasures, its own ends."[12] This very direct articulation of the notion of separation moves to the fundamentalist impulse that shapes the Left Behind viewpoint. The wheat and the tares (translated "weeds" in the RSV) are destined to be separated.

Seen in this light, the doctrine of the Rapture appears to be more than a simple matter of interpreting key biblical passages. Separation from the world is a foundational mindset that was present at the time of the formation of dispensationalism and continues to be a driving force that directs the way the biblical text is handled. For LaHaye and Jenkins the Rapture is part of a comprehensive worldview, a complete paradigm that, once entered, has an answer for everything in its self-contained world. If the Rapture is not clearly taught in Scripture it must be posited in the gaps.

In the parable of the weeds (unbelievers) and wheat (believers), both "grow together until the harvest" (Matt 13:30). Contrary to what pretribulational advocates maintain, the tares are dealt with first, "Gather the weeds first and bind them in bundles to be burned, but gather the wheat into my barn" (Matt 13:30). As Gary DeMar points out,

> C. I. Scofield, author of the notes in the _Scofield Reference Bible,_ reverses the order: "At the end of this age (v. 40) the tares are set apart for burning, but _first the wheat is gathered_ into the barn (John 14:3; 1 Thess 4:14-17)." Why is Scofield's view so important? Almost every modern-day advocate of the pretribulation rapture, LaHaye included, is indebted to Scofield in some way. In order to make his prophetic system work, Scofield must reverse the clear order of events in Mathew 13:30.[13]

It would seem that commitment to the dispensational system has precedence over the biblical text itself.

The brief consideration of the biblical passages just quoted reveals the focus of the New Testament. The Resurrection is inextricably linked with the presentation of the second coming of Christ. The front side of the Second Coming is heralded by the resurrection of Christ. The earliest preaching of the apostles proclaimed, "in Jesus the resurrection from the dead" (Acts 4:2). The astounding news of the apostles was that the resurrection, which was expected to occur at the end of time, had transpired in their lifetime! As N. T. Wright puts it, "The one true God had done for Jesus of Nazareth, in the middle of time, what Saul had thought he was going to do for Israel at the end of time."[14] Saul had thought that God would vindicate *Israel* after her suffering at the hands of pagans, but instead God vindicated *Jesus* at the hands of pagans. Saul had thought that the great reversal, the great apocalyptic action, would take place at the end of time with a flourish of divine intervention on behalf of Israel. In truth, the great reversal, the great Resurrection, had happened in one man. To preach that the resurrection of the dead had begun in Jesus is to say that the crucified and risen one is the central figure of God's saving action.

Even as the resurrection of Jesus Christ marks out the culmination of God's saving history, so it also heralds the onset of the new aeon. The line of argumentation set out in 1 Corinthians is unmistakable; since Christ has risen from the dead, so we too can expect to be raised on the Last Day. The vindication of Jesus as the Messiah of God is not complete until those who belong to Christ are also raised from the dead. The second coming of Christ is the event at which the graves of the righteous and the unrighteous shall be opened, "all who are in the tombs will hear his voice and come forth" (John 5:28-29). In Jesus' death and resurrection the Age to Come had already arrived, and on the basis of that great reversal, all life is changed.

When one begins to view the death and resurrection of Jesus Christ as the central organizing event of Scripture, it becomes possible to clear away some additional problems of terminology that cloud the issue. According to LaHaye, "The Blessed Hope" of Christians is the pretribulation rapture of the church. He makes much of this little phrase that is found in Titus 2:13. It is a verbal marker or cue that calls to mind the dispensational system he sets out. But is LaHaye's assertion true to what the book of Titus is speaking about? The passage in question reads, "awaiting our blessed hope, the appearing of the glory of our great God and Savior Jesus Christ." As LaHaye would have it, this short phrase is referring to two events: the blessed hope, and the great appearing of the Lord. The Left Behind series is based on this distinction for all the events in the twelve books—the great tribulation, the rise of the Antichrist, the rebuilding of the temple, everything from Revelation 4–19—are made to fit between the blessed hope and the great appearing.

The "Blessed Hope," according to LaHaye, is a pretribulation rapture of church out of the world. The reason it is blessed, one is left to assume, has to do with the fact that, according to Left Behind, believers will not have to suffer the tribulation. They will not be there. That may be a happy thought, but Scripture does not promise that the church will not have suffering or will be spared tribulation. It would certainly make light of the suffering of today's persecuted church around the world to say such a thing. The "Blessed Hope" is not the avoidance of difficulty but precisely the overcoming of all opposition in the victory of Jesus that finds its fulfillment at his return. His work of judgment and redemption will be fulfilled at that time. We will all be present for that ultimate reality. The blessed hope is not separate from but synonymous with the second coming of the Lord of heaven and earth.

Left Behind as a Closed System

How is it possible for so many concerned Christians to have such distinctive views? What makes the secret rapture of the church a compelling doctrine and a plausible starting point for the Left Behind series? Given a discussion of the texts such as we have just undertaken, one would think that support for a doctrine that is not expressly taught in Scripture would lose its attraction. Yet, it seems to remain as a position many are willing to acknowledge if not embrace. A few are even willing to defend the position. So how is it that such a state of affairs can be accounted for?

Of all the arguments that could be marshaled, it should not be overlooked that the secret Rapture doctrine is taught to millions of conservative Christians in churches large and small. The power of having this teaching as one's own default position must be reckoned with. When the 1 Thessalonians passage is read in a dispensational context, the expected scenario is rehearsed as an accepted expression of religious imagination. The sociology of knowledge makes acceptable the questionable interpretation and indeed makes it the only officially received position within that given congregation. It is unlikely that a layperson would challenge the reading or point out that the doctrine was unknown in the church before the nineteenth century.

Not long ago, I had lunch with a colleague of mine. She is an accomplished professor, lecturer, author, foreign missionary, and for years has cohosted a very popular radio program. Having grown up in a dispensational church she could speak from experience as she informed me, "Dispensationalism was the eleventh commandment." At an early age the Rapture doctrine was a part of her thinking as well as the various dispensations and very particular views on the book of Revelation. "By age fourteen I had given up on the system, and I didn't go back to a reading of Revelation until my twenties." My colleague no longer sees things as a dispensationalist, but it required a paradigm shift to move her from her childhood views. That speaks to the power of communal knowledge and what we might call "default position."

Classic dispensationalism is a complete system of theology as comprehensive in its dimensions as Arminianism, Calvinism, or Lutheranism. It has a great deal of internal cohesion, and as with any system of thought has answers to objections put to the system. When one thinks according to the system, scriptural interpretations buttress and support other aspects of the presentation. One portion of the system comes to the aid of the other. That is characteristic of any system of theology. In the case of dispensationalism, this is all the more true because of the structure given to this form of thought by its first exponents and by certain interpretive positions of the system.

The high degree of cohesiveness found in the system is due to Darby and Scofield. As trained lawyers who both practiced law during their respective careers, they exercised considerable skill in logically ordering the complicated system of dispensational thinking. Codifying the curious hermeneutical positions and the famous end time calendar in the Scofield notes to the Bible, dispensational-ism gained an enviable consistency among member's allegiance. But cohesiveness is not the same as faithfulness with regard to the text of Scripture, as we have seen. And in the tug-of-war between the system and the text, it would seem that the system wins more often than the text.[15]

One reason this is so has to do with dispensational hermeneutics, the science of interpreting Scripture. On the surface the appeal is made to the "plain" meaning of the text. Irene's populist stance was adduced at the beginning of the chapter to show that the Left Behind point of view wants to claim final authority for the text of Scripture. This is an admirable position. As LaHaye puts it, "When the plain sense of Scripture makes common sense, seek no other sense, but take every word at its primary, literal meaning unless the facts of the immediate context clearly indicate otherwise."[16] What at first blush sounds so good and reasonable turns out to be very different in practice. It should not be overlooked that the "plain" or "literal" meaning of the text as set out in the Left Behind series is anything but "plain" and is certainly not "literal."

Standing underneath the "plain" meaning of the text are a whole set of presuppositions that dictate certain outcomes. In an earlier chapter it was pointed out that the Left Behind point of view dis-tinguishes whether a text is meant for a Jew, a Gentile, or is meant for believers. This artificial starting point leads to scores of distinc-tions in handling the text of Scripture. For example, the kingdom of God and the kingdom of heaven are distinguished on the basis of this hermeneutical principle. The Rapture is distinguished from the glorious appearing of Christ, even though there is no reason to make a distinction based on the terminology of the New Testament. The church and Israel are so separated that they become two peoples of God. What is "plain" or "literal" in one way of thinking is clearly not so in another.

In addition to these distinctions, we also find a second herme-neutical procedure that complicates the handling of Scripture. Many prophetic texts are said to have an earthly fulfillment for

Israel and a spiritual fulfillment for the church. Where the first procedure tends to make distinctions where there are none, the second makes multiple levels of meaning out of a single text. With the expanding of options by which one may interpret a passage, there is also increased ability to harmonize in a way that promotes the appearance of consistency. But what one really sees is a closed system.

The closed nature of the system can be seen by the way in which arguments are made for the doctrine of the Rapture. Tim LaHaye asserts that the Rapture is one of eleven mysteries unknown to the Old Testament saints that is now revealed in the New Testament.[17] He alludes to the doctrine by calling to mind three key passages: 1 Thessalonians 4:13-18; 1 Corinthians 15:51-53; and John 14:1-3. But there is precious little exposition of these texts and no explanation that takes into consideration the different historical settings represented, or the diverse theological points being addressed. By combining these three passages LaHaye derives a sequence of events that he places on a chart for ease of understanding.[18]

LaHaye simply asserts that the rapture of the church and the glorious appearing, or revelation of Christ, are not the same event. We are assured by LaHaye that "These two episodes, the Rapture and the Second Coming are so different that it is impossible to combine them."[19] One is left to assume that LaHaye's word is all that is necessary in the matter. In place of biblical interpretation one is given a rather haphazard populist reading that divines a sequence of events without reference to the rest of Scripture. Historical and exegetical research is bypassed for the familiarity of a populist reading of the text that reaffirms dispensational positions.

Mark Hitchcock and Thomas Ice argue in much the same way in their book *The Truth Behind Left Behind*. As they point out, the term "rapture" is not found in the text of Scripture but the concept of "catching up" is present in 1 Thessalonians 4. This proves that the Rapture or "catching up" is biblical! This is an astounding piece of logic, but apparently it is enough for them to establish the mere term "rapture" without going into any unpleasant details. This populist approach to Scripture continues as Hitchcock and Ice cite three authors who disagree with dispensational doctrine. What is interesting is that there is no engagement with the objections of those cited.[20] It's as though Hitchcock and Ice speak a different language. Alluding to the "plain" meaning of the text as they understand it is a sufficient proof to their way of thinking. Hitchcock and Ice seem absolutely oblivious to the fact that scores of historic premillennialists also affirm a "catching up" of believers in the air but do not regard this as something other than the second coming of Christ.

LaHaye, as well as Hitchcock and Ice, divide Scriptures into two sets: one that describes the Rapture, the other which depicts the glorious appearing. This is an example of making a distinction where there is none. In this scheme Scriptures having to do with the catching up of the church are separated from Scriptures having to do with the manifestation or revealing of Christ in his power. But as George Eldon Ladd points out, the vocabulary used of the Lord's return does not support the idea of two comings of Christ, or of two aspects of his coming.[21] Whether Scripture speaks of the Lord's coming (_parousia_), or his revelation (_apokalypsis_), or his manifestation (_epiphaneia_), it refers to one glorious event.

A basic contradiction appears when one looks closely at the lists just described. If Scripture is read in a literal manner, we would expect that 1 Corinthians 15 would refer to Christ's glorious appearing since it speaks of the "last" trumpet. This, however, is not the case. Instead, we find that LaHaye unashamedly insists that the "last trumpet" of 1 Corinthians 15 describes the pretribulational rapture of the church. Seven years after the "last trumpet" sounds, another trumpet is sounded at the visible second coming of Christ (Matt 24:31). Hence, the trumpet sound described in 1 Corinthians 15:51-53 is not the _last_ trumpet

There are many obvious problems in reconciling the two sides of LaHaye's list, but of course, there is a ready answer. We are informed that when 1 Corinthians 15 says "the _last_ trumpet" it really means the last trumpet for the church. This is not to be confused with the seventh trumpet of Revelation 11:15 which is _really_ the last trumpet of God's saving plan. In this case one has to ask what a literal interpretation of 1 Corinthians 15:51-53 might mean? Apparently it means reading the text with an Israel/church distinction already in mind. Or, another way of putting it is to say one must view the text according to the dispensational structure of thought. That is the true test of what is "literal."

What is just as interesting as the contradictory content of these positions is the manner of the argumentation. For when viewed from a particular light, LaHaye's argument is really no argument at all but an assertion of dispensational presuppositions. Hitchcock and Ice fair no better. They seem quite unwilling or unable to speak to the concerns of those who do not view Scripture from a dispensational vantage point.

No one can be the servant of two masters. Either the one will be loved and the other despised, or the second will be loved and the first despised. In its attempt to proceed with twin commitments to the dispensational system and to a literal reading of the Bible, it would seem that the reading of Scripture sometimes takes a backseat to the system. As we have seen, asserting the secret rapture of the church in light of what Scripture actually says is hard work. One might well imagine that the impossibility of the task would give rise to second thoughts among dispensationalists. But what gives life to the enterprise is the system that includes certain nonnegotiables. Items such as the Rapture and a seven year tribulation are the presumed world of discourse. These familiar landmarks of the Left Behind point of view, as well as many others, are read into the text as though they always belonged there. This is a circumstance in which the system fairs much better than the text of Scripture, revealing a biblical hermeneutic that reads Scripture with a particular end time calendar in view.

Dispensationalism stands or falls as a complete system of thought. As such, it is a closed system that has taken pains to teach and defend the cogency of each particular within the system. Scripture has been interpreted so as to assure and affirm the elements of the construct developed by Darby and Scofield. There is a consistent internal logic with Scriptures lined up in a manner that affirms the whole. The system itself is what gives meaning and value to various events in the Bible and events of the day. The world makes sense when viewed in this way. Seeing things differently would require a paradigm shift. Perhaps that is why it is so difficult for LaHaye or Hitchcock and Ice to mount a meaningful argument. That would require stepping out of the mindset of dispensationalism to engage someone from a different point of view.

The Vision of the Redeemed Future

The vision of the redeemed future set out in Scripture has its culmination in the revelation of Jesus Christ. The object and focus of that unfolding story is the sovereign Lord of the universe, the savior, redeemer, the shepherd of his people, the slain one, the judge of the nations, the giver of forgiveness of sins who is coming again. Titus 2:11-14 tells us that, "the grace of God has appeared for the salvation of all men, training us to renounce irreligion and worldly passions, and to live sober, upright, and godly lives in this world, awaiting our blessed hope, the appearing of the glory of our great God a Savior Jesus Christ, who gave himself for us to redeem us from all iniquity and to purify for himself a people of his own who are zealous for good deeds." When this vision is reclaimed we will find certain consequences follow in its path.

First, we will gain the big picture for God's plan for the universe. Instead of being squeezed into an end times calendar according to modern proponents of prophecy teaching, we will be allowed to see the great vista and expansive hope toward which we are moving. Or perhaps better, we will become attuned to the salvation of Jesus Christ that is rushing toward us out of God's future. The expansive vision is the proper antidote to the narrowing tendency of the closed interpretive system of dispensationalism.

Second, we need to see that passages as diverse as Isaiah 65, Romans 8, 1 Thessalonians 4, 1 Corinthians 15, Revelation 21 and 22 all view the same reality using differing language and different images.

This frees us to allow the language of Scripture to function in the manner in which it was meant. For example, we are not obligated to make the false distinction between the "coming" of the Lord and his "appearing" as though these are two distinct and separate events. Scripture passages that speak of his appearing (e.g., 1 Thess 3:13) cannot be pitted against those that speak of his coming (e.g., 1 Thess 4). To do so does violence to the way that the language of the Bible functions. Both texts have to do with the second coming of Christ. Reclaiming the grand sweep of God's salvation will allow the language of Scripture, in all its variation, to paint us a full image of the day of the Lord. This will keep us from allowing lesser pictures of the end to occupy our imaginations.

Third, allowing the vision of the redeemed future to dominate our thinking on these matters allows us to set aside false dualisms of various kinds to focus on the redemption of creation. The Left Behind series does not think in terms of creation but finds ways, because of the pervasive dualism that it participates in, to break apart what God has kept together. The interpretational presuppositions demand a separation between Jew and Gentile, Israel and the church, the believer and the unbeliever, heaven and earth, and the list goes on. This organizing principle (or should we say separating principle?) strains to the breaking point the Bible's narrative account of God's dealing with the nation of Israel, the coming of the Messiah, and the inauguration of the new eon in the resurrection of Jesus Christ.

When Scripture speaks of the return of the Lord, it is filled with the awesome reality of God's power and judgment. Only as he establishes his justice will all things be made right. But the proclamation of Scripture is not meant to drive to fear or to be obsessed with the signs of the times. The return of the Lord is the blessed hope of the believer. "For God has not destined us for wrath, but to obtain salvation through our Lord Jesus Christ, who died for us so that whether we wake or sleep we might live with him" (1 Thess 5:9-10).

Chapter 4

Israel:
God's People or God's Time Clock?

Fascination with Israel and Jerusalem stand at the heart of dispensational prophetic teaching. One can hardly overestimate the importance of Israel as God's time clock for the events leading up to the age to come. In the early years of dispensationalism there was fascination over and support for the Zionist movement. The belief that a regathered Israel played a role in end times prophecy also led to missions to evangelize Jews. Fascination turned to elation as the nation of Israel was formed in 1948. And all eyes were riveted upon the Middle East in 1967 as the Six-Day War brought Jerusalem, with its temple precinct, into Jewish hands for the first time since the Babylonian captivity. These events are not viewed by dispensationalists as the product of mere chance or the twisting caprice of blind history. All these events, we are informed, were foretold in the pages of Scripture and are the anticipated outcome of biblical prophecy.

The focus placed on Israel and Jerusalem in dispensational thought thus goes beyond fascination to what we might call expectation. The dispensational system was and is built on the anticipation that before any of the prophesied end times events can take place, Jews must be reestablished once again in the Holy Land. As Timothy Weber puts it, "Without a restored Jewish state, there could be no Antichrist, no great tribulation, no battle of Armageddon, and no second coming."[1]

In short, everything is riding on belief in the Jewish people in a restored Jewish nation. The role of Israel in LaHaye's form of biblical prophecy is so dominating that it effectively recasts the message of the Bible placing the words of Jesus, the message of Paul, and entire narrative of God's dealing with Israel in the Old Testament in its debt. The theology of large portions of Scripture is overshadowed in the effort to give an account of Israel in an end times calendar and to tell the story of how the world will come to an end.

Tim LaHaye can raise the issue of the importance that Israel plays in end times prophecy in a rather nonchalant manner by merely asking a question: "Has it ever seemed strange to you that almost every night on the evening news the eyes of the world focus on a little country of five million people in the Middle East?"[2] This common sense approach, typical of prophecy teachers, links current events with biblical prophecy in a very accessible way. With equal ease, it is pointed out that the Jewish people have retained their identity for centuries without a homeland. The Hittites are gone, the Assyrians and the Babylonians are vanished—but the Jewish people continue! Could that have occurred without some special providence of God? There is so much attention on the little country in the Middle East, LaHaye asserts, simply because the prophets had so much to say about Israel and Jerusalem.

Perhaps at this juncture we should adduce that age-old adage that says there is no such thing as a free lunch. Such an easy movement from biblical text to current events must have its price. What is the cost? How far have the biblical texts been pushed to achieve this particular reading? If Israel is so important for end time prophecy, why is it that the New Testament writers do not directly say so? The apostle Paul does not go on about the nation of Israel as the key for biblical prophecy. LaHaye and Jenkins produce some texts from the gospels that purportedly show Israel in certain terms, but that is by no means clear. We will take a closer look at some of these texts in what follows. But for the time being it is enough to simply ask the question, "How do we know that Israel plays the role in future events that is set out in the Left Behind series?"

Many readers of the Left Behind series may not be aware of the presuppositions and social factors that are assumed by the Left Behind series. The dispensational system has particular ways of reading and interpreting biblical texts. These "ground rules" have important consequences that dictate certain outcomes. That is the topic of this chapter. We will proceed by hearing what LaHaye and Jenkins have to say about the role of Israel in biblical prophecy. As we discuss a few of the important biblical texts on this topic we will be asking the question: "Does the Bible place modern-day Israel at the center of biblical prophecy?" Next we will make explicit those presuppositions and social factors that have a strong effect on the dispensational interpretation of Scripture. Finally, we will end with a brief word making a case for one people of God and not two. I hope to show that in order to bring current events into sharp focus for an end times calendar, the biblical text has been forced to say something that it doesn't.

Some Biblical Considerations

LaHaye is quite emphatic: Israel is the focus of world attention and is the object of biblical prophecy. The assertion could not be expressed any more confidently when he says, "I call the regathering of five million Jews back to the Holy Land and their becoming a nation in our generation 'the infallible sign' of the approach of the end times."[3] LaHaye approvingly cites John Walvoord, past president of Dallas Theological Seminary and prophecy teacher when he says:

> Of the many peculiar phenomena which characterize the present generation, few events can claim equal significance as far as Biblical prophecy is concerned with that of the return of Israel to their land. It constitutes a preparation for the end of the age, the setting for the coming of the Lord for His church, and the fulfillment of Israel's prophetic destiny. Israel, God's "super-sign" of the end times, is a clear indicator that time is growing short. God is preparing the world for the final events leading up to Israel's national regeneration.[4]

LaHaye is convinced, as are other dispensationalists, that the miraculous return of the Jews to their homeland is the most significant end times event that has transpired in the last twenty centuries. One might even call it a "super-sign."

According to LaHaye there are three miracles that mark, or will mark, the progress of the regathered nation. The very existence of the Jews and the Jewish nation is the first miracle. The second is the possession of Jerusalem for the first time since the Babylonian captivity. The third has to do with the nation of Israel experiencing a great spiritual awakening. This will occur when the Jews accept Jesus as their Messiah, the very one they rejected in the first century.[5] This event takes place in *Soul Harvest,* the fourth book of the Left Behind series. This last miracle is the only part of the threefold miracle that has not yet come true.[6]

Where does LaHaye turn for the scriptural support for his assertion that Israel stands at the center of biblical prophecy? Interestingly enough, Ezekiel 37 with its vision of the dry bones is chosen. In this passage, Ezekiel the prophet was brought out in the Spirit and set down in the middle of a valley full of dry bones and asked if these dry bones could live again.

> So I prophesied as I was commanded; and as I prophesied, there was a noise, and behold, a rattling; and the bones came together, bone to its bone. And as I looked, there were sinews on them, and flesh had come upon them, and skin had covered them; but there was no breath in them. Then he said to me, "Prophesy to the breath, prophesy, son of man, and say to the breath, Thus says the Lord God: Come from the four winds, O Breath, and breathe upon these slain, that they may live." So I prophesied as he commanded me, and the breath came into them, and they lived, and stood upon their feet, an exceedingly great host.
>
> Then he said to me, "Son of man, these bones are the whole house of Israel. Behold, they say, 'Our bones are dried up, and our hope is lost; we are clean cut off.' . . .
>
> Then say to them, Thus says the Lord God: Behold, I will take the people of Israel from the nations among which they have gone, and will gather them from all sides, and bring them to their own land; and I will make them one nation in the land, upon the mountains

of Israel; and one king shall be king over them all; and they shall be no longer divided into two kingdoms. They shall not defile themselves any more with their idols and their detestable things, or with any of their transgressions; but I will save them from all the backslidings in which they have sinned, and will cleanse them; and they shall be my people, and I will be their God." (Ezek 37:7-11; 21-23)

This prophecy was delivered to the people of Israel in exile. The nation had been conquered by the Babylonians and in a series of deportations had been carried away to a foreign land. First Israel and then Judah were taken from the Holy Land given by God. As the prophecy indicates, they were indeed a people without hope. The rich themes of faithfulness in the face of faithlessness, redemption, return, and kingship are explored in this prophecy.

Yet these are not the themes LaHaye finds important. There is only one matter that takes up his attention while looking at this text. As LaHaye explains:

> The gradual growth of the Israeli nation from scattered skeleton to full body development is startling. As Ezekiel's prophecy indicates: "There was a noise, and . . . a shaking, and the bones came together, bone to his bone" (37:7, KJV). Following this, "the sinews and the flesh came up upon them, and the skin covered them above: but there was *no breath* in them" (37:8, KJV, emphasis added). From the sound of an earthshaking event (World War I), the seemingly dead nation of Israel was to *gradually* formulate a body, *after* which the spirit would be breathed into it. We submit that history records the birth of the nation of Israel exactly in this manner, beginning in 1917.[7]

The breath that is to be blown into the body is what LaHaye takes to be a great awakening of faith produced by the Spirit (breath or wind) of God. So it is that he can say that Israel is only a "breath" away from fulfilling this prophecy.

At least two points of clarification are in order. How is it that LaHaye can take Ezekiel 37 for a prophecy about modern-day Israel when the vast majority of biblical scholars say the passage was fulfilled when Israel returned to the Holy Land under the leadership of Nehemiah circa 538 BC? The rebuilding of the temple under Nehemiah came after the Babylonian captivity during which Ezekiel's prophecy was given. It would seem the sequence most scholars give to these events is correct. LaHaye avoids this interpretation by saying that the land promises to Israel have not yet been fulfilled. The promise of the return to the land is not fulfilled in Ezekiel's time because the return did not retrieve Israelites from global dispersion.

Perhaps the best way to explain this issue is to turn to yet another passage. In Isaiah 11:11-12, the prophet says the following:

> In that day the Lord will extend his hand yet a second time to recover the remnant which is left of his people, from Assyria, from Egypt, from Pathros, from Ethiopia, from Elam, from Shinar, from Hamath, and from the coastlands of the sea. He will raise an ensign for the nations, and will assemble the outcasts of Israel, and gather the dispersed of Judah from the four corners of the earth.

Since the return of the Jews from the Babylonian captivity to their homeland under Nehemiah was from one country to another, from Babylon to Israel, it does not qualify as gathering the nation "from the four corners of the earth." Since that return did not retrieve Israelites from global dispersion as the formation of the modern-day Israel did, fulfillment must be found in our modern circumstance. Therefore, the prophecy of Ezekiel 37 can only apply to the modern-day nation of Israel.

The second point of clarification has to do with the importance of World War I in LaHaye's explanation of the Ezekiel prophecy. It may seem odd that mention of a twentieth-century event would play so prominently in the interpretation of a biblical text from the exilic period. And indeed, we have already seen the unusual way in which these texts are handled for the purpose of making connection between current events and biblical passages, but for LaHaye the regathering of the modern nation of Israel must be dated from

World War I. LaHaye, it would seem, takes delight in telling how the Balfour Declaration stating the British approval of a homeland for Jews was signed in 1917, in the midst of the Great War. Why World War I? Once again, it is because the Bible foretold the event through prophecy. LaHaye is convinced that a special kind of war—a world war—will mark the time of the end.

The prophecy in question is found in Matthew 24:7-8, which reads in the following manner, "For nation will rise against nation, and kingdom against kingdom, and there will be famines and earthquakes in various places. All these things are but the beginning of the birth pains" (ESV) The birth pains that initiate the end times will be marked by a war that is started by two nations followed by a quick escalation that sees surrounding kingdoms joining until the whole world is involved. When this takes place you have *the sign.*

> We submit that is exactly what occurred in June 1914 when the Archduke of Austria, Prince Francis Ferdinand, was shot by a Serbian zealot in the very area of the world where in these days UN peacekeepers must be stationed to keep the Serbs and Croats from killing each other. One month later Austria declared war on Serbia, followed shortly by the other kingdoms of the world, until all but seven nations officially joined the conflict (and even the seven "neutral" countries sent mercenaries).[8]

In addition, LaHaye points to the flu epidemic of 1918 and famine that followed in the wake of the Great War for the fulfillment of the rest of the Matthew passage.

Childbirth brings about many birth pains. That is why LaHaye goes on to warn those who discount World War I and its subsequent catastrophes as the fulfillment of "the sign." While it is true that the Great War was not the war to end all wars, and only twenty-two years later the world was thrown into World War II, the issue is one of timing. "World War I did not signal that we should look for the immediate coming of Christ or 'the end of the age.' It signaled that we should look for more birth pains."[9] This move allows LaHaye to read into the Ezekiel passage the "noise and shaking" of World War

I, to keep the door open for further birth pains, and to keep the return of the Lord imminent.

The clarifications of these two points begin to demonstrate the convoluted manner in which Scripture is used in the dispensational point of view. It is clear that the great advantage of this approach of reading the texts is that it allows the maximum exchange between the Bible and our twenty-first century circumstance. But in an effort to read the signs of the times, the texts are divorced from their own historical context. The Bible is thus read as a book written entirely to modern people, and not to the original readers. The text of Scripture is not the source for but the occasion of finding the predetermined outcome dictated by the dispensational prophetic system.

Ezekiel 37 has nothing to do with the formation of the modern nation of Israel, and everything to do with the return of Israel to the Holy Land after the Babylonian captivity. One only needs to read the passage in its historical context. The revelation of God given to Ezekiel took place at a time when the nation of Israel was overrun by the Babylonians. The prophet was himself deported and thus felt the sting of exile. The most natural understanding of the word of God given to Ezekiel in chapter 37 is that it refers to the return of the Jewish people after seventy years of captivity (Jer 25:11-12; Dan 9:2). The solemn promise that God made to the people when he said, "I will bring you in to the land of Israel" (Ezek 37:12) was fulfilled at the end of the seventy years. There is thus good reason why most of the church disagrees with the fanciful Left Behind scheme that sees modern-day Israel at the center of predictive biblical prophecy.

How about the land promises? Are they still waiting to be fulfilled? Isn't that good warrant for seeing Isaiah 11 as a promise for the regathering of Israel? The passage does speak of the Lord extending his hand a second time to recover the remnant of his people "from the four corners of the earth." But once again, all one needs to do is to turn to a recognized commentary to find a sensitive treatment of the passage. What are the two times referring to? The allusion is to the rescue from Egypt when the Lord, with a strong right arm and an outstretched hand, brought deliverance to his people. The "second time" would thus be the return of Israel from her dispersion among the nations—from Babylon—and is not a reference to two future regatherings, one before and one after the tribulation as LaHaye would have us believe. Further, the prophet Isaiah is not saying that the earth has four corners. It is also a very forced reading that would require "four corners of the earth" to mean "global" in a sense only open to moderns, or to render it as the central or key meaning of this text.

According to the Left Behind point of view, Israel's past restorations did not ultimately fulfill the land promises given to Abraham, Isaac, and Jacob. This is the basis upon which Ezekiel 37 and Isaiah 11 can be urged upon the public as proof that the modern nation of Israel is relevant to biblical prophecy. But this seems to be in contradiction with important Scriptures. Joshua 21:43 reads, "the LORD gave to Israel all the land that he swore to give to their fathers; having taken possession of it, they settled there." Again in the same chapter we read, "Not one of all the good promises which the LORD had made to the house of Israel had failed; all came to pass" (21:45). In the book of Nehemiah we have recorded, "and thou didst find his heart faithful before thee, and didst make with him the covenant to give to his descendants the land of the Canaanite, the Hittite, and Amorite, the Perizzite, the Jebusite, and the Girgashite; and thou hast fulfilled they promise, for thou art righteous (Neh 9:8). Scripture is quite certain on the point; the land promises have been fulfilled. To assert otherwise is a curious position indeed.

What about seeing World War I in the Matthew passage? Clearly the modern nation of Israel was formed in 1948, and with some historical latitude one could say that the Balfour Declaration could mark the beginning, moving the date to 1917. And clearly the Matthew passage speaks of wars and rumors of wars. But to connect the two occurrences can only be accomplished through sleight of hand. The text simply does not describe World War I. It does fit the context of Matthew's own community. The first century was indeed a time of wars of all kinds in the outer realms of the Roman Empire. There were disturbances in Germany, Gaul, Armenia, and other locations. Wars of various sorts were being waged. Nation against nation, kingdom against kingdom describes what indeed was taking place. That phrase does not and cannot be shorthand for a special kind of war. The text simply cannot bear that freight. It does, however, describe the "Messianic Woes" that will accompany the end of the age. The birth pangs of the age to come will shortly be upon them, and for this reason they must not be deceived. The crucifixion and resurrection of Jesus as well as the destruction of Jerusalem in AD 70 will all be accomplished in their lifetime.

The parable of the fig tree is another favorite passage of those who put great stock in the regathering of Israel as the infallible sign of the end times. "From the fig tree learn its lesson: as soon as its branch becomes tender and puts forth its leaves, you know that summer is near. So also, when you see all these things, you know that he is near, at the very gates. Truly, I say to you, this generation will not pass away till all these things take place" (Matt 24:32-34). Left Behind adherents think they see the nation of Israel in this passage. "When we see the rise of the nation of Israel as a nation (as we did in 1948), we will know that the time of the end is 'near-at-the-doors.'"[10] LaHaye asserts that the symbol of the fig tree usually refers to Israel and leads him to believe that we are in the season of our Lord's coming. Apparently, the formation of the modern nation of Israel corresponds to the fig tree putting out leaves. This assures those who are watching that the signs have been fulfilled.

One question remains: what generation is being referred to as Jesus speaks these words? It would seem that whatever generation he had in mind would not pass away until all these things occurred. For Tim LaHaye and the Left Behind series the things that are to occur are nothing less than the beginning of the end. The secret rapture starts the time clock ticking again, followed by the tribulation, the revealing of the Antichrist, the battle of Armageddon, the glorious appearing, the millennium, and the great white throne judgment. But which generation will see these things? Four options are laid out by LaHaye:

1. *The disciples' generation.* But nothing like this happened historically during their lifetime. Their generation has passed, and the Lord has not yet come, so it doesn't seem possible He had the disciples' generation in mind.
2. *The generation that saw World War I.* It was thought by many fine Bible teachers to be a possibility. That scenario becomes increasingly unlikely today because most of that generation has already passed away. Still, the unlikely possibility that "this generation" means the generation that saw World War I should not be ruled out completely for another five years or so.
3. *The generation that saw Israel officially become a nation in 1948.* That generation was old enough to "see" the United Nations officially recognize Israel as a nation. Assuming this generation includes children ten years of age or older in 1948, it probably means the generation born around 1938—give or take five or ten years.
4. *The generation that lived through the Six-Day War of 1967.* That war took place when the Israeli army marched into Jerusalem and raised its flag over the city. This would mean the generation born around 1957.[11]

These four options, we are told, hold the key to the timing of the prophecy of Matthew 24.

Gary DeMar points out that LaHaye has not been consistent on this point. In the first edition of his *Beginning of the End* (1972), LaHaye chose option number two, the generation that saw World War I. However, in the revised 1991 edition, option number two no longer looks as good to LaHaye, who now claims that option number three is most likely. DeMar notes matter-of-factly that "This change gives LaHaye another fifty years before this new generation passes away."[12]

Indeed, the shifting of positions is not limited to the two editions just cited, but extends to his more recent book entitled, *Are We Living in the End Times?* (1999). Speaking to the matter of the critical or strategic generation, LaHaye offers the following common sense word: "One thing is for sure: It's dangerous to be dogmatic! Which is why we prefer to say we believe 'this generation' refers to those alive in 1948. It may, however, mean those alive in 1967 or those alive during some yet future war when the Jews will once again gain total control of their holy city."[13] In other words, LaHaye is saying that it could be option two, three, four, or an option not as yet written. The flexibility of this statement illustrates one of the social aspects of this kind of end time teaching: it appeals to populist interpretations of reality, so it must remain adaptable to changing circumstance.

This offer of "choices" can hardly promote confidence in LaHaye's point of view. One is left to assume, upon reading such a statement from LaHaye, that five or ten years from now there may be another list of options to choose from to determine what "this generation" means. In fact we can be assured of that. As those who were alive at the time of World War I pass away, option number two will have to be deleted, but as we have been reminded, we cannot rule it out altogether for another five years or so. When this is finally done it will be one more instance in which the original prophecy has been traded in for a new version. In this example, we have been told that the formation of the modern nation of Israel is the "super-sign" of the end days. "This generation" refers to the generation alive at the time of the founding of Israel. LaHaye marks this event from the signing of the Balfour Declaration in 1917.

On the surface, LaHaye's comment that we should not be dogmatic about prophecy pronouncements seems generous and self-effacing. LaHaye seems reasonable and moderate in asserting that one must not be more specific in one's interpretation than the prophecy is in itself. Who wants to be accused of time setting? We all know that no one knows the day or time (Matt 24:36; Mark 13:32). But the "flex factor" that is built into the Left Behind approach allows the signs and symbols to alter while simultaneously holding to a rigid prophetic outlook that holds the Bible and its meaning hostage to the tyranny and clamor of current events.

LaHaye's comments seem self-effacing but only prove that his form of apocalyptic thinking has an agenda that is quite unperturbed by the text.

So what are we to make of Matthew 24 and our discussion of "this generation"? How can we determine who Jesus was speaking to? This is a key question for the Left Behind point of view. The sliding scale of options that LaHaye offers is not the only way this question has been answered. Saying that Jesus is referring to a future and as yet unknown generation is not the only or the best solution. It would seem that LaHaye's presuppositions force him to look for an answer in the future. Does the text suggest or require this conclusion? What would a first-century audience have understood Jesus to mean by his sayings? A host of biblical expositors are convinced that Jesus is speaking to the disciples' generation and not to a future generation.

Gary DeMar, in his critique of the Left Behind series, takes the time to give a brief account of Matthew 24. In his view it is only by dealing with the entire chapter that the subject can be treated in an adequate manner. His approach attempts to deal with these passages with sensitivity to people of that time. Instead of isolating a verse and giving it a meaning that applies to current events, DeMar seeks to read the chapter with a larger frame of reference. Surely the utterances of Jesus would have had significance to those living at the time. If so, how would they have heard the message of Matthew 24?

At the beginning of the chapter Jesus predicts the destruction of the temple. Pointing to the impressive stonework of the building he says, "You see all these, do you not? Truly, I say to you, there will not be left here one stone upon another, that will not be thrown down" (Matt 24:2). In the Roman invasion that took place in AD 70 the temple was indeed destroyed. DeMar points out that Jesus was speaking about the temple that stood before them at that time. His concern was to alert them to what would happen in their lifetime, not what would happen at the site of some future rebuilt temple.

The unexpected words of Jesus then caused the disciples to approach him privately to ask a series of three questions. "Tell us, when will this be, and what will be the sign of your coming and of the close of the age?" (Matt 24:3b). The disciples were quite clear on the fact that the destruction of the temple could only mean one thing: the end of the age. This is not the same as the end of the world. Such a notion would not have entered their minds. What would have immediately registered in their thinking is the transition that all Jews were expecting from the old covenant to the new. Jeremiah 31 had spoken of the new covenant and the renewal of God's people. And his prophecy was only one of many regarding the new age. But the arrival of that new age meant the coming of the judgment of God that was necessary to bring about the end of this age, the close of the old in favor of the new.

The age to come is marked by the centrality of the work of Christ. He is the one in whom the covenant is fulfilled. As the writer of the book of Hebrews puts it, the old covenant is obsolete in light of the new (Heb 8:13). The work of Christ resulted in the "age to come," which incorporated believing Jews and Gentiles into the blessings of Jesus' blood (Luke 22:20; cf. Jer 31:31; Acts 10; Rom 9–11; 1 Cor 11:25; 2 Cor 3:6; Eph 2; Heb 8:8, 13). DeMar goes on to say the following:

> Jesus replaced the sacrificial system of bulls and goats with Himself as the "Lamb of God" (John 1:29), the physical temple with "the temple of his body" (John 2:13-22), a sanctuary built with hands with the "true tabernacle" (Heb 8:2; 9:11, 24), and God's earthly, sinful high priest with Himself as the "perfect high Priest" (Heb 2:17; 3:1; 5:1-10; 7:26-28). That was why Paul could write that "the end of the ages" had come in his day (1 Cor 10:11; cf. Heb 1:1-2). The "end of the age" refers to the last days of the old covenant world that were passing away (1 Cor 2:6). The destruction of the temple was the observable sign that the end was a reality and the new covenant had dawned.[14]

The point that DeMar makes so well is that Jesus himself, in his life, ministry, death, and resurrection, brings in the new age. This is the reality of which he speaks in the Olivet discourse. The object of Jesus' sayings in Matthew 24 has to do with the age to come, not the end of the world, and certainly not with a fanciful end times calendar.

DeMar's exposition is to show that all the signs spoken of in Matthew 24 were fulfilled in the first century. As he puts it, "From persecution and tribulation to earthquakes and famines, Jesus' prophetic words were fulfilled to the letter."[15] A first-century hearer would have understood Jesus' sayings in the context of the Jewish hope of the age to come. The temple was indeed destroyed and not one stone was left upon another. The message Jesus gave in the Olivet discourse was directed to the disciples' generation. DeMar warns that if we abandon the clear texts and their historical fulfillment then they can be applied to any generation, the very thing that LaHaye and Jenkins do in the Left Behind series.

N. T. Wright, a prodigious New Testament scholar, sees the matter in a similar fashion. Wright is convinced that the words of Jesus recorded in Matthew 24 and the parallel passages in Mark 13 and Luke 21 refer to the coming destruction of Jerusalem. This position clearly stands opposed to the Left Behind point of view but is also carefully worked out by Wright in dialogue with liberal and conservative authors.

On the liberal end of the spectrum Albert Schweitzer, that famous humanitarian and New Testament scholar, suggested early in the twentieth century the idea that Jesus was an apocalyptic teacher. By that he meant that Jesus predicted the end of the world within a generation. According to Schweitzer, because the end of the world did not come to pass as predicted, Jesus was a failed prophet. Other scholars, believing that Jesus never would have said anything about the end of the world, decided that those passages dealing with apocalyptic teaching were the invention of the early church and not original to Jesus. Even many popular readings within conservative circles have said something quite similar. Thinking that Jesus had predicted the end of the world, and that it did not happen within a generation, he must have meant something else by "this generation."

Wright addresses this problem by saying that the persistent misreading of these passages can be solved only when we have a proper appreciation of the prophetic ministry of Jesus. The kingdom of God was the central concern of Jewish life in the first century. When Jesus came teaching in the countryside his message was not a collection of abstract truths of universal applicability reminiscent of certain forms of Deism. His was a message of the vindication of Israel, the defeat of evil and victory over the pagans, and the establishment of peace and justice. All this was to be accomplished by Israel's God who would rouse himself and reveal himself as the ruler of the universe.

The hope of Israel's vindication could be framed in the language of a new exodus. God had saved Israel before, more than once through exodus. The first exodus from Egypt was followed by exodus from Babylon. Now in the time of Roman oppression, the Jewish people continued to recount the many ways in which YHWH had shown himself to be king, both of Israel and of the whole world. Jesus undertook the telling of this Jewish story in his own time as a prophet. The coming of the kingdom had to be accompanied with both words of judgment and the offer of welcome into the kingdom.

Wright stresses that Jesus' Jewish contemporaries who were looking for the appearing of the kingdom were not looking for anything like the end of the world or what has been called a "cosmic meltdown." They were, Wright insists, expecting a great event that would mark the beginning of something new for Israel. The mighty event was to usher in the climax of Israel's history, but this new reality would have its effect within the created world as we know it. Precisely because of the "newness" of the event, end-of-the-world language is the only set of metaphors adequate to carry the significance of what will happen. References to heaven and earth passing away are not meant to be read any more literally than the prophecies of Isaiah and Jeremiah who use the same kind of end-of-the-world language to refer to events surrounding catastrophic events in the history of Israel.

The key then for reading Mark 13, Matthew 24, and Luke 21 is to see that Jesus is in fact predicting the fall of Jerusalem. Jesus' prophetic ministry led him to speak openly about how Israel's long exile was finally coming to its close; but additionally it led him to speak subversively about how the present regime in Jerusalem stood against the holy purposes of God and was subject to divine judgment. As Wright puts it:

> Already present in Jesus' ministry, and climactically inaugurated in his death and resurrection, the divine kingdom will be manifest within a generation, when Jesus and his followers are vindicated in and through the destruction of Jerusalem. The generation that rejects Jesus must be the last before the great cataclysm. There can be no other, because if there were they would need another warning prophet; once the father has sent the son to the vineyard, he can send nobody else. To reject the son is to reject the last chance.[16]

Thus, the prophecy to "this generation" is thoroughly comprehensible in the context of the prophetic ministry of Jesus. The prediction of the fall of Jerusalem has theological significance. That has not always been seen, and is given as one of the reasons why the obvious way of reading the text has been ignored. But if Jerusalem is seen as the seat of opposition to the God of Israel it becomes quite clear that the "this generation" is the generation of the disciples who were also vindicated at the time of Jesus' resurrection.

Left Behind's easy movement from current events to the biblical text comes at a very high price. If we take a moment to gather up some of the insights of the proceeding pages, this becomes clear. If we recall the discussion regarding Ezekiel 37 and the valley of dry bones, we see that there is no particular attempt by LaHaye to read the text in its most obvious sense. Ezekiel 37 has nothing to do with the modern state of Israel and everything to do with the return from the Babylonian captivity. The text is pushed into the background as other interests take charge. In the case of Matthew 24:7-8 and the discussion regarding nation rising up against nation, it must be said that the creativity in reading World War I into that text is breathtaking. This is such a classic case of reading into the text that it is hard to take seriously. And finally, the case of determining what "this generation" might mean also takes us rather wide of the text itself. LaHaye's position, replete with marking out several options that have yet to be written, exposes his disregard for the clear meaning of the text.

Presuppositions and Social Factors

What are we to make of this? Why is the text of Scripture left behind in the effort to establish the modern nation of Israel at the center of biblical prophecy? It causes one to wonder what kind of forces or presuppositions are at work to drive this agenda forward. I suggest that there are several factors at work, quite separate from the text, which motivate the Left Behind point of view. There are both social forces and theological choices that cluster around issues important at the time of the formation of the dispensational point of view and that continue to be factors in the present.

On the matter of social forces Vern Poythress is very helpful. In his book *Understanding Dispensationalists,* three sets of social factors that contribute to a unified dispensational reading of biblical texts are set forward. The first of these has to do with the manner in which dispensationalism gave answer to Darwinism. In the face of the exaltation of science as the arbiter of a human worldview, dispensationalists set out the Bible as the source of truth. As we have seen from the earlier historical sketch of the movement, biblical prophecy played a particular role in validating the truth claims of Scripture. "Hence there is pressure on dispensationalists to believe the Bible has a great deal of precision in its language and to interpret its language in the least figurative way possible."[17]

The second factor has to do with fear of subjectivity. Dispensationalists have been suspicious of the interpretations of mainline denominational teachers. They see in the modern church setting a throwing over of the cardinal truths of the faith. LaHaye traces the defection in doctrine to Modernism arising after the Civil War. As it infiltrated denominations, subjectivism became rampant. "Today these 'mainline' churches, as they like to call themselves, have lost touch with mainline Christian doctrine."[18] In place of this kind of harmful subjectivity, dispensationalists appeal to the "plain" meaning of the text. This is a populist move away from the authorities—in this case the mainline teachers—who have led the people in the wrong direction. To appeal to the "plain" meaning of the text sounds more objective. But whether or not the populist interpretation of a biblical text is any more reliable is another matter.

The third social factor has to do with the apparent lack of reflection on the matter of hermeneutics—the science of interpretation—which leads dispensationalists to read the Bible as though there are no social factors involved in reading the text. Poythress puts it in the following manner:

> When we advise the average readers of the Bible that the meaning is "plain," what will they conclude? They will tend *not* to read it in its original historical context but in the context of the twentieth century, their own subcultural context. The Bible is thus regarded as a book written directly to modern people, not mainly to the original readers. Who, then, are the modern people whom the Bible addresses? Most immediately they are the circle of Christians within which a dispensationalist moves. To lay dispensationalists "plain" meaning is meaning that they automatically see in a text when they read it against the background of the teaching and examples that they have seen and heard from fellow Christians, most of whom are themselves dispensationalists. "Plain meaning" can all too easily become, in practice, the meaning of a text when seen through the framework of the dispensationalist system—or any other system for that matter.[19]

Of course the critique of reading the Bible without adequate recourse to the original historical context is one that could be brought to quite a number of nondispensationalist Christians. In the case of dispensationalism, however, the social factors are amplified.

Within dispensational churches both large and small, the emphasis on the "plain" meaning usually works to discourage pastors from alerting their congregants that there may be other interpretations. Additionally, in accordance with social factor number one, if someone deviates from dispensationalist teaching, it may be seen as a liberalizing tendency or worse—a repudiation of the Bible that goes against the "plain" meaning of the text. But here it must be seen that the "plain" meaning of the text has been established and confirmed within the confines of a particular social group.

The power of the social force within dispensationalism to unify the reading of biblical texts should not be underestimated. Classic dispensationalism is a complete theological frame of reference that possesses inner coherence. Scripture passages are explained in such a manner that each has its place in confirming the dispensational understanding of things. There are also answers to standard objections ready at hand. If one had been taught dispensationalism from childhood, knowing no other way of reading the text, it would take nothing short of a paradigm shift for one to embrace a different view of end times.

One senses the social factors at work in the explanations and rebuttals given by Mark Hitchcock and Thomas Ice as they attempt to substantiate the truth behind the Left Behind series. We have already seen in their affirmation of the doctrine of the secret rapture of the church that there was no attempt to clarify the cultural setting of the biblical text(s) in question. For them it was enough to assert that the term "rapture" is found in any number of commentaries that they possess. This argument is no argument at all for one who stands outside the dispensational system. But for those who are a part of the insider group, we are left to assume, this is enough of an appeal to the "plain meaning" of the text to satisfy populist need.

Again, in the instance of the place of modern-day Israel in biblical prophecy, we find Hitchcock and Ice giving a "nonargument argument" that amounts to reasserting the claim made in dispensationalism that the land promise to Israel was not fulfilled. There is no discussion of Ezekiel 37, the key passage in the dispute. Neither is any attempt made to refute the evidence given by DeMar, though he is mentioned by name. An explanation of Isaiah 11:11-12 is offered, and the final summary is given. "This text only permits two worldwide regatherings from *the four corners of the earth*. Therefore, the present Jewish State *is* very relevant to Bible prophecy."[20] Standing behind this line of argumentation is the dispensational adherence to the "plain meaning" of the text, but quite tellingly there is no discussion of the cultural setting in which Isaiah is writing.

When one turns to a recognized commentary, a very different explanation of the same passage is given. When Isaiah says, "The Lord will extend his hand yet a second time to recover the remnant that remains of his people," the question naturally arises, "What was the first occasion on which the Lord extended his hand to recover his people?" The allusion is to the rescue from Egypt when the Lord, with a strong right arm and an outstretched hand, brought deliverance to his people. The "second time" would thus be the return of Israel from her dispersion among the nations—from Babylon—and has wider allusions to the Messianic kingdom to come but is not a reference to two future regatherings as dispensationalist teaching would have it.[21]

As strong and influential as social factors may be in providing a unified reading of biblical texts among dispensationalists, there is a fundamental theological presupposition that drives the case. The present Jewish State is at the center of dispensational notions of biblical prophecy because it was placed there at the founding of the movement. From J. N. Darby and C. I. Scofield to Hal Lindsey and Tim LaHaye there are two people of God and thus two purposes of God. God's dealing with the nation of Israel is described for us in the pages of the Old Testament. But when Jesus came and his own people did not accept him the prophetic time clock stopped. God turned from dealing with the people of Israel and thus the "church age" began. The so-called parenthesis theory has Christ dealing with the church in anticipation of the moment in which the prophetic time clock starts running again. Only after the secret rapture of the church will God's saving purposes for the Jewish people be restarted. The vector of salvation goes in only one direction.

One People of God

Recently I was teaching a seminar consisting of pastors and laity. In the group was a pastor friend of mine who is a convinced dispensationalist although most of his congregation is not. I was teaching about the saving work of Jesus Christ and the fact that all the promises of God find their "yes" in him (2 Cor 1:20). He is the center and meaning of all of history—the one who is worthy to open the scroll because he "didst ransom men for God from every tribe and tongue and people and nation" (Rev 5:9). I went on describing how the death and resurrection of Christ broke down the dividing wall between Jews and Gentiles that he "might reconcile us both to God in one body through the cross" (Eph 2:16). Even as Old Testament believers looked to the future for the fulfillment of God's promises which took place in Jesus Christ, so we too in the New Testament era look back on the work of God in Christ as fulfilled in accordance with Scripture. In other words, the saving work of Christ is the centerpiece of human history, creating one people of God to the glory of Father, Son, and Holy Spirit.

At this point in the presentation, as I was showing how the two vectors—one future looking, one backward looking—embrace all history, my friend's eyes got very wide. Without warning he blurted out, "No wonder my people (who are not dispensational in outlook) don't get excited when I start talking about the Second Coming!" He didn't stipulate precisely as to which aspect of dispensational thought they took umbrage with, but it could have been the fact that according to dispensational thinking, the saving vectors only go in one direction. Because Old Testament saints are not a part of the church, they do not receive the same spiritual benefits. Israel is not the people of God, but God's time clock.

But if we take seriously the vision of the promise of God to Abraham, there is another outcome that allows us to keep whole what the Left Behind series breaks apart. The apostle Paul puts it in a surprising way when he says, "The promise to Abraham and his descendants, that they should inherit the world, did not come through the law but through the righteousness of faith" (Rom 4:13). Normally when we think about the promise given to Abraham it is that he should receive a bit of land in what is presently called the Middle East. But notice how the apostle enlarges that vision. It is as though, looking out on the cosmic significance and world-changing significance of the death and resurrection of Jesus, Paul is realizing that the original promise to Abraham of land is a metaphor for what is turning out to be something very much larger. The inheritance of the Old Testament saints together with the New Testament saints ("his descendants") is nothing less than the new heavens and new earth spoken of in Isaiah 65, Romans 8, and Revelation 21 and 22.

It is instructive to see how the apostle deals with the promise given to Abraham. He does not object that the "land promise" has not been fulfilled, nor does he assert that there must be two regatherings of the nation of Israel whether in belief or unbelief. That interpretation of the texts would be too literalistic. Such a reading of events would be too narrow for Saint Paul. On the contrary, his vision of the future is as wide as the promise of God found in Jesus Christ. This vision of God's future smashes through the convoluted end times calendar put forward in the Left Behind series and opens out onto a view of the end that is infinitely more appealing.

Or again, if we turn to Romans 11, we find the apostle Paul teaching the unity of believers of all ages. God has not rejected the Jewish people, but in this passage Paul is wrestling with the difficult concept that some of his people have stumbled so that the whole world would be reconciled—that Gentiles might be included in the people of God.

> But if some of the branches were broken off, and you, a wild olive shoot, were grafted in their place to share the richness of the olive tree, do not boast over the branches. If you do boast, remember it is not you that support the root, but the root that supports you. You will say, "Branches were broken off so that I might be grafted in." That is true. They were broken off because of their unbelief, but you stand fast only through faith. So do not become proud, but stand in awe. For if God did not spare the natural branches, neither will he spare you. (Rom 11:17-21)

The image he uses is an olive tree. The tree is Israel (Jer 11:16; Isa 17:4-6). The natural branches that are broken off are unbelieving Israelites (Rom 11:17, 20). The good branches that remain are believing Israelites (vv. 17-18). The wild branches that are grafted into the good olive tree are believing Gentiles (vv. 17, 19). In this teaching the apostle is clearly working with an understanding that the promises of God apply to both Jews and Gentiles. There is only one tree consisting of those who believe. The true Israel of God, believing Jews, are joined by believing Gentiles into the one tree. There is no evidence here of there being two peoples of God. There is one body of Christ—the church—made up of believers from Old and New Testaments.

The unity of believers taught here and elsewhere in Scripture calls into question the very foundations upon which the Left Behind series is based. Not to recognize Old Testament believers as part of the one family of God makes of Israel something she is not—God's time clock as opposed to God's people of faith. To posit two different ways of dealing with true believers before the time of Christ and after the time of Christ is outside the framework of Scripture. When one begins to see that the promises of God are for the whole people of God, it makes the confused and fragmented system of secret rapture and separate dealing with natural Israel replete with renewed Old Testament sacrifices seem like a bad dream.

Chapter 5

The Subtle Dangers of End Times Teaching

Ideas have consequences. Take an example from the history of medicine: early Americans from the 1700s believed that the oils of their skin kept them from getting diseases. As a consequence they bathed very infrequently, thinking that "overwashing" would make them more susceptible to the threat of infection. They had a corresponding need for deodorizing herbs and plants to offset the naturally accumulating aromas of the body. All this may seem odd to us. Deviation from frequent baths or showers that most Americans have come to expect as normal can only be seen as odd, barbaric, or illogical. But to the early Americans it made perfect sense.

There is more. When dealing with an infection or disease, doctors of the day relied upon time-honored views of the Greeks. Galen (200–129 BC), a well-respected practitioner of the Hippocratic oath, set forward the philosopher's system of four bodily humors: blood, yellow bile, black bile, and phlegm. These were identified with the four elements (fire, water, earth, and air) as well as the four seasons (spring, summer, fall, and winter). Quite often, when someone was afflicted with disease or fever, the recommended treatment consisted of bloodletting. Balancing the humors was thought to be key in relieving the symptoms. Later, new views on how pathogens are spread to humans led to the eventual abandonment of bloodletting as a treatment and the development of alternative interventions. But while medical opinion viewed the world from the vantage of humors and their control, bloodletting made perfect sense. Ideas do have consequences.

The Left Behind point of view is an aggressive millennial view that has consequences. We have already seen that there are very distinct theological positions that are dictated, such as the premillennial or secret rapture of the church, and the radical separation of Israel and the church with respect to the promises of God. There are the ancillary commitments to biblical predictions of World War I and the formation of the modern state of Israel standing at the heart of their view of biblical prophecy. And of course, there is the very specific end time calendar beginning with rapture, tribulation, revealing of the Antichrist, rebuilding of the temple and reestablishment of sacrifices, the glorious appearing, the millennium, the last rebellion, the great white throne judgment, and the eternal state. These views in themselves have implications and consequences that may not always be attached to what many see as being "the truth about the end." But as we continue our look at the Left Behind point of view, certain questions arise. What are the ethical implications and commitments of the Left Behind point of view? What kinds of actions flow out of a commitment to this particular apocalyptic view of the end of the world? That is the subject of this chapter.

In order to be complete, the answers would have to be as comprehensive and contradictory as life itself. That is clearly not possible. But in what follows I would like to trace a few areas in which outcomes flow as a consequence from the dispensational premillennial thought forms. These all have ethical implications, and in some instances can be linked to specific actions of religious and often political significance. The first area of consideration is the millennial mindset, which tends toward insider information, conspiracy theories, and a very particular way of interpreting the world.

Second to be considered are some consequences of this millennial mindset, such as the use of fear as motivation, an essential fatalism that dictates one's approach to political issues in the Middle East, and the labeling of people groups that is endemic to the dispensational point of view. Finally, we turn to a brief consideration of the ethical issues that surround the dispensational support for rebuilding the temple in Jerusalem. Here we will find that the Left Behind point of view has associated itself with some of the most dangerous and extreme elements of Israeli society.

Millennial Mindset

Timothy Weber, in his study on dispensationalism, points out that the group has always exhibited a strange blend of activism and passivity. Critics charge that the essential pessimism of their teaching relegated dispensationalists to the sidelines as observers of the end times calendar. Human civilization is doomed to decline, religious interests are mired in a growing apostasy, and worldwide deception at the hands of the Antichrist is a certainty; nothing can change the profile of the world gone bad because of sin. It leaves the convinced dispensationalist in a place where nothing can be done to change these unalterable truths.[1]

Logically speaking, this outline does take away the motivation for ethical action in the world. But things are never as simple as they appear at first glance. It is true that dispensationalists are convinced that the world is on a slippery slope to destruction. No amount of human effort will be able to bring about peace. No matter how noble the cause or brilliant the plan, the downward trajectory cannot be stopped. But for all that, dispensationalists did find reason to become engaged in various causes and actions thus, in part, escaping the charge of complete passivity.

Early on it was said that dispensational pessimism cut the nerve for evangelization. If Christ was returning "any day," where is the opportunity to organize and promote revivalism? What is the use of planning for the future if the future is liable to be cut short? And yet, dispensationalism managed to turn this disadvantage to good use, by saying that since time is short, believers needed to warn as many as they can. Thus the "any day" character of the Rapture became motivation for evangelism.

It was also asserted that the pessimistic worldview would undermine the necessity for working for social welfare and foreign missions. While many were passive in the face of great needs on these two fronts, there were also many who engaged in remarkable ways. Nineteenth-century foreign mission endeavor was based on the prevailing postmillennial thought that the world would be Christianized before Christ's return. Dispensationalists agreed that someday soon Jesus would rule over the earth, but disagreed with the idea that this would be brought about by Christian cooperation. At base dispensational missions and social efforts were not motivated by the benevolent empire model but belief in a cataclysmic intervention by the returning Christ. In this they were similar to the Millerites, who also had a pessimistic view of history. "Dispensationalists developed a logic of their own that allowed them both to give up on the world and to engage it simultaneously."[2]

To explain this phenomenon, Timothy Weber writes:

> Believing that Jesus could come at any time was not the same as believing that he would arrive on a particular day. Instead of grappling with the ramifications of a definite date for Jesus' return, dispensationalists learned to live with a new sense of urgency about present tasks. Because there was the possibility that not much time was left, believers needed to get serious about their Christian responsibilities.[3]

Since they were living in the "great parenthesis," life could not be organized around a specific date. The driving force of dispensational motivation is found in two mutually conditioning beliefs: the uncertainty of the day of the Lord's return coupled with the belief that it would be soon.

In the early decades of the twentieth century, dispensationalists were content to sit on the sidelines, teach their doctrine, look for signs of the times, and find special meaning in the current events of the daily newspapers. But since the reestablishment of Israel, there has developed an ever-increasing apocalyptic fervor among dispensationalists. The older approach that was content to assert that God alone had to bring the end time prophecies to pass is giving way to the desire to become more involved. While dispensationalists of the past were satisfied to watch world events from seats in the bleachers, now they are becoming players on the world stage. With increased political clout and a vastly improved network from which to effect change, dispensationalists are doing precisely that. Some would even say they are helping prophecy along.

In addition to the historical and theological factors we have been considering, some recent studies on apocalyptic or catastrophic millennialism may also shed light on the ethical consequences of the Left Behind point of view. There are characteristics and tendencies of the millennial mindset that may help to place our discussion in context.

There is no disputing the fact that the Left Behind point of view has its face fully turned toward the future. Tim LaHaye asserts that these are the most exciting days in which to live, not only because of great technological advances, but, more important, because "we twenty-first-century Christians have more reason than any generation before us to believe that Christ will return to take us to His Father's house."[4] LaHaye takes great delight in pointing out that almost thirty percent of Scripture is dedicated to Bible prophecy.

Further, the Left Behind point of view presupposes that Bible prophecy is meant for new believers. The proof given is that one of the first New Testament books, 1 Thessalonians, is full of teaching about the Second Coming, the Rapture, the Antichrist, the wrath to come, and other future events. Even if one buys into LaHaye's understanding of the Rapture, it does sound somewhat odd to make such a blanket argument about the centrality of Bible prophecy for Christian living. Surely LaHaye is not suggesting that a new believer getting ready for his or her first Easter celebration should sit down and study out such issues as the Gog-Magog battle, the rebuilding of the temple, and the place of Babylon in Bible prophecy (assuming one believed in the dispensational accounts of these events). Or is he? Prophecy is so important to the Left Behind point of view, one wonders.

What yields the answers to life's most pressing questions? You guessed it—Bible prophecy! This is how LaHaye and Jenkins put it: "Failure to understand God's plan, from the coming of the 'first Adam' to the second coming of Christ to establish His kingdom, will keep you from answering the big philosophical questions in life: *Why am I here? Where am I going? How do I get there?* Only a study of prophecy adequately answers all of these questions."[5] This startling assertion, as it stands, would be rejected by the overwhelming consensus of the Christian tradition. These questions have not been absent from the discourse of the church. There has been a long and distinguished record of dealing with these questions through Christian theology and philosophy. Christian prophecy does have its place, but it is by no means what is central.

Yet, when understood from the point of view of an aggressive millennial mindset it makes perfect sense. The *only* answer for the big questions of our time and of our individual lives comes from the millennial worldview of the speaker. The apocalyptic vision of dispensational premillennialism offers a reading of the future as though it were history written in advance. It alone renders understandable the confusing array of historical events and movements that threaten or seem to threaten the faithful remnant. By being apprised as to how God will act to bring the age to a close, one is given opportunity to prepare for the final onslaught. There is comfort and a degree of control in wrestling with the ambiguities of a complex and rapidly changing sociological situation when armed with special knowledge.

Bernard McGinn, an expert on apocalyptic discourse, summarizes the orientation of groups and movements that are focused on the end times under three points. Apocalyptic texts from various religious backgrounds and different ages display family resemblances in key areas that include: 1) a sense of the unity and structure of history conceived as a divinely predetermined totality; 2) pessimism about the present and conviction of its imminent crisis; and 3) belief in the proximate judgment of evil and triumph of the good, the element of vindication.[6] The Left Behind point of view fits this description perfectly.

Richard Landes, in his article on millennialism for the _Encyclopedia of World Religions_, offers a few more characteristics of apocalyptic millennialism. He says that these millennial "believers find themselves at the very center of the ultimate universal drama and their every act has cosmic significance."[7] He explains that it is not unusual for believers in this heightened state of anticipation to begin to find cosmic messages in the smallest incident. Believers become "semiotically aroused" as they see evidence of their imminent vindication all around them. In the case of the Millerites, certain biblical prophecies all lined up to yield the year 1843. In addition, at the beginning of that fateful year a large comet blazed across the northern skies. Some in the movement gave it little credence, but many believers and near believers knew this celestial sign to be further "proof" of Father Miller's prediction that Jesus Christ would return in 1843.[8]

In the case of the Left Behind point of view there are abundant examples of how the millennial mindset sees special proof for reading the world in a particular way. Take for example LaHaye's treatment of the Gog-Magog war that is supposed to precede the Rapture. Ezekiel 38 and 39 constitute a prophecy that Ezekiel is to pronounce against Gog. It is a passage that LaHaye interprets as referring to an end time invasion of Israel by a Russian army. "Etymologically, the Gog and Magog of Ezekiel 38 and 39 can only mean modern-day Russia."[9] On this point LaHaye is following the party line of dispensationalism from C. I. Scofield through Hal Lindsey. Ezekiel's reference to Meshech and Tubal is taken to be an exact correspondence to Moscow and Tobolsk. And the reference to Rosh is taken to refer to Russia. But the etymological "proof" offered up by LaHaye has no substance at all.[10] As the premillennialist Ralph Alexander comments, "Some understand _rosh_ to mean modern Russia, but this identity has no basis. Those holding such a view appeal to etymology based on similar sounds . . . but such etymological procedure is not linguistically sound at all. The term Russia is a late eleventh-century-AD term."[11] This does not daunt the apocalyptic mindset of LaHaye and Jenkins. What is more important than what the Scripture says is the role that countries play in the end time calendar.

As LaHaye goes on to explain, Russia has only a short time to fulfill her role in Bible prophecy. But ever since the fall of the Berlin Wall and the breakup of the Soviet Union, Russia has been getting weaker not stronger. The economy is in shambles and the military is compromised. As LaHaye speculates, "If Russia is to attack Israel, she had better do it soon!"[12] Either Russia must strike Israel or she will be thrown onto the economic trash bin of history. At her present rate of decline, LaHaye thinks there may be anywhere from five to twenty years in which to fulfill prophecy.

If one has not given up on the hopeless logic of LaHaye's rhetoric, it has the force of heightening expectation. This thing must happen soon and then the rest of the sequence outlined in the Left Behind scenario should follow hard on its heels. The prediction has been specific enough to increase urgency, yet there is what one might call a strategic ambiguity that keeps the prediction outside the reach of being disproved. This allows a probability factor to remain for those who do not need convincing to remain in the fold.

But precisely at this point, LaHaye makes an astounding statement: "Warheads are known to have a seven-year shelf life; they will be dead in their silos before another decade passes, and Russia would no longer be able to fulfill prophecy."[13] How are we to read this utterance? Is LaHaye indicating his preference for a shorter timeline? Or is he giving room to the possibility that Russia might not in the end fulfill her prophetic role? This is an odd way to argue and one can only speculate that should Russia devolve further in power that LaHaye and others may well have to come up with a new interpretation for Ezekiel 38 and 39. That is an eventuality that I am sure they will be happy to accommodate.

Stranger still is the way LaHaye ends his explanation of these things, saying only, "Just one more reason for believing Christ could come in our generation." This seems to be the mantra that recurs again and again. When referring to the Arabs and Jews being at the center of the world's stage he says almost cheerfully, "Just as the Bible said they would be." And when asking, "How close are we?" with respect to the rebuilding of the temple, he launches into a familiar saying. "We have more reason to believe Christ could return in our lifetime than any generation before us!" This statement is a tautology; any generation could say the same. Yet, in the rhetoric of apocalyptic millennialism it must be heard to say, "Any Day!" This is an intoxicating message that puts the believing hearer at the center of ultimate reality, able to discern with accuracy the meaning of each passing incident.

Listen to LaHaye as he gives meaning to the rebuilding of Babylon. The ancient empire, as with so many other matters in the Left Behind point of view, plays an important role in Bible prophecy. According to LaHaye, "You can be sure that any city mentioned seven times in two chapters, as is Babylon in Revelation 17 and 18, will be a literal city."[14] We are assured that this rebuilt city of Babylon will become Satan's headquarters, serving as the governmental and commercial capital of the world during the first half of the tribulation. These are general "facts" that are given to us. But what is really important for us to know is not understood, generally speaking, in the West.

According to LaHaye, Saddam Hussein started the Gulf War in order to aggrandize himself. His real plan was to control the world through oil. He failed when his friend Russia would not or could not neutralize the West and permit him to carry out his plans. LaHaye continues:

> Religiously, Saddam may give lip service to Muhammad and act like a devoted Muslim, but there is strong indication that he is actually a Satanist. A key is found in Dr. Charles Pak's report of his 1975 visit to Babylon to witness firsthand the rebuilding of that ancient city. There, for the first time in his life, Dr. Pak witnessed the worship of the devil at a reconstructed temple to the sun. When you recall that Hussein is known to micromanage everything in his

country, including that entire rebuilding project, you can be sure that a temple to Satan would not be there without his approval.[15]

This insider information is served up with references to official reports and personal visits by dispensationalist teachers. The narrative makes mention of what "Many Westerners still don't understand" and an important "key" to understanding Saddam Hussein religiously speaking. The tone of LaHaye's explanations seems circumspect. But the sources for LaHaye's insights, not surprisingly, come from other dispensational end times teachers. The plausibility factor forms a rhetorical umbrella over the exciting and exceedingly populist information imparted.

LaHaye continues his account of Saddam Hussein and his meaning for our time in the following selection:

> Saddam Hussein's abnormal hatred for the Jews, Jesus Christ, His followers, and anyone else who would stand in the way of his goal to conquer the world, might best be understood by demonic possession—a virtual foretaste of the Antichrist to follow, who will be indwelt by Satan himself.
>
> In any event, there is little doubt that Saddam Hussein sees himself as the replacement for Nebuchadnezzar, as the man whose destiny it is to rule the world. Of course, he is not fit for such an exalted position; in fact, he is little more than a cheap imitation of Nebuchadnezzar. He could well be, however, the forerunner of the one who we believe is soon going to emerge on the world scene to take control of the United Nations (or its successor), move the commercial and governmental headquarters of his world government to Babylon, and rule the world from what we call in our Left Behind novels "New Babylon."[16]

This presentation is remarkable for a number of reasons.

Apocalyptic millennialism is able to find meaning in unexpected places. To use the phrase of Richard Landes, it is "semiotically aroused." Clearly LaHaye knows something about Hussein that most Westerners don't. For years Western governments dealt with Hussein's administration without being able to penetrate all his motives or his secrets. But for the convinced believer, LaHaye's insight into Saddam Hussein sweeps away any clinging ambiguity and he is able to place his finger on the pulse of palpable evil. There are no shadows or grey areas in the light of this apocalyptic insight. Without ever explicitly saying it, LaHaye has called Hussein demon possessed. Without ever asserting it, LaHaye claims that Saddam Hussein is the forerunner of the Antichrist—whatever that may mean. Innuendo and allusion can do a great deal in the hands of the adept.

This interpretation of Saddam Hussein is an example of one form of Christian apocalyptic. Here we find LaHaye viewing the Iraqi leader as a prototype or image of the final decisive battle between the forces of good and evil. It is also a way for the Left Behind point of view to project its fears and hatreds. There can be hardly anything worse than deception and apostasy. But that is precisely what we find at work in the Satan-worshiping Nebuchadnezzar of our own time. The signs, symbols, and imagery of Bible prophecy are easily exchanged in order to intensify the conflict, magnifying the political reality into a larger frame of reference. Saddam is a figure of importance on the world stage. But, even more important, he plays a role on the stage of Bible prophecy!

Also remarkable is the fact that there will be no need to revisit this flash of insight now that Saddam has been tried and hanged before a court in his own country. Nothing will need to be retracted or retraced. Who knows? In the next edition of the book, there may be a new leader or movement that will be the occasion for special meaning that will affirm the apocalyptic mindset represented by the Left Behind point of view. Every incident, at least for a short period of time, has importance in the apocalyptic mindset of Left Behind. As Yaakov Ariel has put it, "The theme of the novel notwithstanding, *Left Behind* is not necessarily about the future; it is very much about the present and serves as an excellent source to reveal the evangelical attitudes toward almost all aspects of contemporary culture and world order: from married life to the United Nations."[17]

What we have also seen is that the Left Behind series, for all its talk about the literal interpretation of Scripture, is really not about the text at all. Certain Scripture passages become talking points for what really drives the system—the apocalyptic mindset. What comes out again and again is the heightened sense of expectation regarding the coming of the Lord. It may be uttered as the familiar tautology, "We have more reason to believe Christ could return in our lifetime than any generation before us," or it may come as a special word of proof about Saddam Hussein, or the apostasy of the mainline denominations, or the moral declension within or without our country generally speaking. The particular way of parsing the world scene and assigning meaning is what is at stake with the apocalyptic millennial mindset.

At this point in our discussion we can gather together some of the characteristics of the apocalyptic millennial mindset. In the first instance there is a heightened sense of expectation regarding the return of the Lord. This is translated into a close scrutiny of current events with a view to relating it to the Bible. While there are allusions to the Bible passages to establish the Left Behind point of view, the approach to the text is of a very populist sort—what one author has called a "subliminal hermeneutic."[18] Reading between the lines and according to dispensational presuppositions allows the prophecies of Left Behind to be applied to contemporary events, thus increasing the urgency of the prophetic utterances. Concentration on these events causes the true believers to become "semiotically aroused," finding meaning in the most unexpected places. But for all the uncertainty that the world may evoke with its ever increasing evil, the true believer has insider information and "knows" what will happen next. Reading the future like history allows the Left Behind point of view to balance present evil with the certainty of God's ultimate control in the end.

The millennial mindset becomes a platform from which everything else draws its meaning. The mental pathways that mark this mindset constitute a hermeneutic of suspicion that, when applied to current events, reveal the true believer to be isolated from the evil of the world at large and yet on the side of God's unstoppable prophetic plan for planet earth. The mindset itself has ethical consequences of tremendous proportions.

Some Consequences

Perhaps now we are ready to ask the question again: what are some of the ethical consequences of adopting the Left Behind point of view? Let me mention two areas that come to mind: millennialism as manipulation and fear as an unworthy motivator.

LaHaye and Jenkins have inflated the role of prophecy, and by heightening expectation have crossed over into a manipulative apocalyptic millennialism. On the simplest level this happens when people are taught that Bible prophecy is the answer to virtually all of life's issues. Executives, blue collar workers, housewives, and students who attend churches that teach the Left Behind point of view, are trained to know all about the Rapture, the tribulation, the revealing of the Antichrist and Armageddon, among other things. Their religious thought world is filled with visions of these events and many more. The Left Behind point of view places high value on studying Bible prophecy. But how central is prophecy? How important is it to be oriented to the signs of the times anyway? Doesn't this apocalyptic millennialism push one out to the edge of Christianity?

The essential pessimism of dispensationalism has its reasons. It should not be seen as destructive in and of itself. It must be remembered that the system of thought we are exploring is at heart a theodicy. Dispensationalists view the world with an astonishing honesty, acknowledging that our world is broken. There is something desperately wrong with it that only God can fix. This kind of honesty must be applauded. It makes infinitely more sense than certain forms of secular millennialism or, for example, a view that suggests that our physical existence misleads us and what is really important is spiritual salvation or enlightenment.

What is disturbing is the fatalism that attends the pessimism. Grace Halsell tells the story of meeting a man named Clyde on a Jerry Falwell trip to the Holy Land. As they engage in conversation, Clyde shows himself to be adept at giving the answers that dispensationalism provides its adherents. Among other issues, the relationship between Israel and Russia is discussed. Because of Bible prophecy

Clyde is convinced that Russia and Israel are and will always remain arch enemies. When Grace is troubled and asks why that must be, pointing out that there are peaceful negotiations underway, Clyde with simple resolve says, "There will be no peace, until Christ returns—and sits on David's throne."[19] Read as simple pessimism, it is bad enough, but if read as fatalism that says we should not even try, that is another matter.

That is precisely the kind of fatalism that seems to be a part of the Left Behind point of view. The Antichrist, when he appears in the first book, manages to deceive and negotiate peace and that is a sign of the end. It is his ability to make peace with a wide range of interests that marks him out as the evil-possessed human of mythic imagination. No one except the Antichrist himself could achieve this kind of cooperation. But the peace that the Antichrist creates is not really peace at all; it is only the calm before the storm. The message of dispensationalism as far as geopolitics is concerned is simple: if you are for peace initiatives—especially when it has to do with the Middle East—you are on the side of the Antichrist!

Fear plays a significant role in the Left Behind point of view—the second area in which the apocalyptic millennialism has some ethical answering to do. Even something as central to Christianity as conversion is affected by the apocalyptic mindset of the Left Behind point of view. The previously discussed urgency presses the sinner's prayer into a millennial shape. Instead of setting out the persuasive character of Christianity as a thought form, the cogency of the person and work of Christ, or making the saving work of God throughout history as the high note of conversion, we find that in the Left Behind mindset conversion is cast exclusively as escape from the wrath to come. As LaHaye puts it, "Accepting Christ's offer of salvation helps you avoid the traumas of the tribulation on earth even as it allows you to enjoy eternity with Christ."[20] In a subtle way, conversion is turned into a form of insurance against the great judgment. Fear of the horrors of the tribulation is an essential tool in the apocalyptic system to motivate sinners to come to Christ. The fear of the Lord is indeed the beginning of wisdom, but can the same be said of the tribulation?

One summer it was my responsibility to teach a combined middle school and high school class at family camp. The students came to me in the early afternoon after sitting in a class on the book of Revelation. Every day they came to my class aggravated and upset. The images of beasts and judgment swirled about their heads in such a way that they simply could not concentrate on the more mundane topic of Paul's missionary journeys. Only after addressing the fears that had been stirred up by the millennial presentation could we proceed to our study. Apocalyptic millennialism stirs up the pot and keeps the emotions flowing, but doesn't this actually drain and enervate believers? Doesn't it keep them from occupying their minds with the complexity of understanding and living our faith?

Support for Israel and the Rebuilding of the Temple

The Left Behind point of view holds out unwavering support for Israel. Since the formation of the nation of Israel is seen as a fulfillment of biblical prophecy, great attention is given to what happens in that small country. The support for Israel from dispensationalists has been both political and spiritual. On the political front, dispensational Christians have gained influence with politicians in Israel and the United States that has affected change in policy and legislation. On the spiritual side of things, this means pro-Israel organizations. These organizations express themselves in many different ways.

The mission statement for Christians for Israel International says, "Christians for Israel is an international spiritual movement of Christians who recognize the return of the Jewish people to Israel as fulfillment of biblical prophecy and a major sign pointing toward the coming of the Lord Jesus Christ." Projects include prayer for the peace of Jerusalem and charitable relief for those suffering from economic hardships and the effects of terrorism and war. Working with other agencies, Christians for Israel has helped over eighty thousand Jews immigrate to Israel. The reader is urged, "You can help us in this exciting fulfillment of biblical prophecy (Isaiah 49:22)." An article on the website asserts that there are five reasons for Christians to support Israel. Reason four reads: "Christians are to support Israel because it brings the blessings of God to them personally."[21]

Support for Israel is framed in the context of living out or fulfilling biblical prophecy. In this case, much of the work looks to help people and retrieve Jews from other countries for the purpose of *aliyah*, or immigration to Israel. Insofar as the work is humanitarian it has a good ethical outcome. But the observation needs to be made that the one-sided support of Israel and the Jews has the glaring omission of any creative or supportive posture toward Arab Christians. Biblical prophecy of the Left Behind sort narrows the field of vision for humanitarian aid to the special people of God. In this scenario, not all people are deserving of care, not even fellow Christians! It would seem that only the people who play a special role in the fulfillment of the end time scenario are recognizable as objects of special concern.

This is a small complaint in comparison with the more ominous connections of dispensationalism. For in the attempt to keep Israel strong and the sequence of prophetic events moving forward, dispensationalism has become associated with some of the most dangerous elements in Israeli society. It is not merely naiveté that makes it so, but the fact that these religious and political groups seem to agree with the dispensationalist beliefs about what is to happen next. The millennial mindset is keenly tuned to the fulfillment of prophecy. By lending their support—both financial and spiritual—to groups that are not afraid to use violence to achieve their ends, they are helping to make prophecy happen.

Tim LaHaye fully expects a new temple to be built in Jerusalem. The first temple was destroyed at the time of the Babylonian captivity in 586 BC and was rebuilt in the time of Nehemiah and Ezra circa 535 BC. The second temple was greatly expanded during the reign of Herod the Great (37–4 BC) and destroyed in AD 70 by the Romans. Since that time the Jews have been without blood sacrifices and synagogue worship has replaced the sacrificial system as set out in the Torah. Talmudic teaching has reflected the new reality and has referred any future temple to the time of the Messiah.

According to the Left Behind point of view, the third temple will be built with the aid of the Antichrist! Timothy Weber summarizes the view succinctly:

> Not long after the Antichrist brings his false peace to the Middle East, he will assist the Jews in building the temple on the Temple Mount, as a symbol of national security and their redemption. Grateful Jews will hail him as their Messiah and commence Old Testament patterns of animal sacrifice. After three and a half years, the Antichrist will betray Israel by entering the restored temple, declaring himself to be God, and demanding worship. This is the ultimate "abomination of desolation" of biblical prophecy. Many Jews will resist such blasphemy, which will provoke the Antichrist to launch the worst holocaust in Jewish history. During the phase of the great tribulation, a missionary force of 144,000 converted Jews will spread the gospel of Jesus and the coming kingdom and will suffer martyrdom for their efforts. Though the Antichrist's power will be formidable, his days will be numbered. God will pour out divine wrath on those who follow the Antichrist, who will be finally defeated by Christ at his second coming. Surviving Jews will hail Jesus as their conquering and true Messiah. King Jesus will then set up his millennial throne in Jerusalem and construct a millennial temple, the fourth and final temple in Israel's history, where Jews and Gentiles will gather to worship in spirit and in truth.[22]

Of course there are many obstacles to the rebuilding of the temple. Most compelling is the fact that the Temple Mount is dominated by the Dome of the Rock and the Al-Aqsa Mosque and is presently administered by Muslim authorities.

This is a fact that has not escaped the notice of the Temple Mount Faithful, one of three Israeli groups that have goals that are similar to the Left Behind point of view. The Temple Mount Faithful is a very small organization that exists for the purpose of "Liberating the Temple Mount from Arab (Islamic) occupation." They believe that the Dome of the Rock and the Al Aqsa mosque were placed on this Jewish holy site as a sign of Islamic conquest. The removal of "these pagan shrines" is necessary to make possible the consecration of the Temple Mount and rebuilding the third temple. Also to be rejected are any so-called peace talks that "result in the dividing of Israel and the breaking of G-d's covenant." The land being referred to here is not just present day Israel but extends eastward to the Euphrates River. "G-d promised to Abraham and to his seed that the land and the borders of Israel are eternal and cannot be divided and given to other people and nations."[23] It only follows that the Temple Mount Faithful would be in support of any and all settlements in the Golan Heights and would completely reject the right of anyone to ask the settlers to leave.

The objectives of the Temple Mount Faithful are framed in religious terminology. But it is interesting to note that neither of the founders of the organization are particularly religious. Stanley Goldfoot emigrated from South Africa to Palestine in the 1930s. A convinced Zionist, he joined the Stern Gang in its fight against the British. The Gang became infamous for its use of assassination, bank robbery, and massacres of Arab men, women, and children. Stern differentiated between "the enemies of Israel" (the British) and "Jew Haters" (the Nazis). He had in mind to stop the former and neutralize the latter. Stern failed in his bid to offer his services to the Axis powers against the British in return for Jewish sovereignty. After Stern was killed during an arrest attempt in 1942, the group reorganized under the name Lehi, which in Hebrew is an anagram for "Fighters for Israel's Freedom."

The next six years saw increased tension and fighting. The number of Jewish settlers had grown exponentially; Palestinian residents felt betrayed by the British and bullied by the burgeoning numbers of their neighbors. In 1948 the U.N. negotiator Count Bernadotte had proposed internationalizing Jerusalem. This attempt to quell the tensions only seemed to fan the flames of trouble. Goldfoot, Lehi's intelligence chief, directed the operation that told the world what Lehi thought about the plan. In his own words, "We decided he was the enemy, and we *executed* him—on the seventeenth of September, at ten past five."[24] Apparently compromise of any sort was not in the Lehi platform. The German machine gun that had been used worked flawlessly. Goldfoot was arrested after the murder but was never charged. Eventually he was released.

In the 1970s Goldfoot published a journal called *The Times of Israel* that by his own estimation was extremely right wing. He also helped to found the Temple Mount Faithful. In the eighties he became involved in a new organization by the name of the Jerusalem Temple Foundation. The board was made up of a number of American dispensationalists, including Terry Reisenhoover, James DeLoach, Doug Kreiger, Charles Monroe, and Hilton Sutton. The Los Angeles-based foundation was formed to provide financial support for the Temple Movement in Israel. Goldfoot's role in the organization was to bring to American Christians a firsthand account of the miracles that God had used to fulfill biblical prophecy to this point. As one who had lived through the formation of Israel, the Six-Day War, and the Yom Kippur War, he could bring an air of authenticity to the subject. His itinerary took him into some of the larger dispensational churches including Chuck Smith's Calvary Temple in California. Some say several million dollars were raised for the rebuilding of the temple and support for the settlement movement.

Gershon Salomon is the aging leader of the Temple Mount Faithful. He served in the Israeli military, and his use of a cane is a reminder of wounds received in a battle with the Syrians. He is perhaps best known for demanding that Muslims be thrown off the Temple Mount. He has stated that, "The Supreme Court should be on the Temple Mount," and, "The Israeli army should parade there."[25] Nothing short of complete Israeli control is acceptable. From Salomon's point of view, any compromise is an offense to the prerogatives of Israeli nationhood. His stance on this point is unwavering and he manages to restate it publicly several times a year. Newspaper ads, street flyers, bullhorns, and confrontation tactics are the methods most often used.

On one such occasion a handful gathers at the ramp that leads to Mughrabi Gate. As they moved forward one of Salomon's followers urges holiday worshipers at the Wall plaza to take the mount from the Muslims; ultra-Orthodox men gathered to argue the point.

> "Until the Messiah comes, it's forbidden to go up there," roars a yeshivah student.
> "You're standing in the Messiah's way," Salomon's man yells.
> "You think this is redemption? Redemption is when you and I overcome our evil impulses."
> "The Temple was always built by human beings."
> "Great sages told them to, not a few media hounds."[26]

This exchange sums up a few of the differences between the secular nationalism of Salomon and the religious Jews who are content to pray at the Wall. For most Jews there is no urgency to rebuild the temple. Jewish faith has been sustained for centuries without animal sacrifices; a return to these bloody practices is not countenanced by many. The synagogue tradition, venerable and certain of itself, is not interested in forcing an issue that could only light a fire in an already smoldering political landscape. But this is not the stance of Salomon. His viewpoint, stemming from an extreme nationalism of soil, myth, and messianism, is not averse to the use of confrontation and even violence to achieve its ends.

On this day the few dozen Salomon supporters are bolstered by scores of evangelical Christians. A pastor and some of his congregants from Florida are in attendance. They, along with many others, are in Jerusalem to attend a Feast of Tabernacles event run by the International Christian Embassy. Formed in 1980, the evangelical organization is pro-Israel, seeking to show love for Israel and to fulfill Zechariah's prophecy that in the Last Days all nations will come to Jerusalem to celebrate Sukkot. The group of one hundred fifty or two hundred people moves up the ramp and is stopped by the standard line given by the police that Salomon has heard numerous times: "I am sorry you cannot enter. The Mount is closed today to visitors."

Salomon takes the megaphone and shouts in English. He speaks of seeing the temple rebuilt soon and of the fulfillment of the end time prophecies contained in Scripture. His wording is precisely what will thrill the hearts of the evangelical Christians in attendance. As Gorenberg wryly comments, "A nationalist in his native tongue, Salomon has absorbed a Last Days vocabulary in English that fits his evangelical audience's expectations."[27] Salomon has courted that portion of evangelicalism that holds to the Left Behind point of view. But perhaps it could be just as accurate to say that evangelicalism has wooed this larger-than-life Zionist.

Pat Robertson has hosted Gershon Salomon on the very popular *700 Club*. Chuck Smith, founder of the Calvary Chapel movement, has met the leader of the Temple Mount Faithful and speaks of "Rabbi Salomon"—a title that would surprise anyone who has paid attention to his political affiliations and dealings. Christian tour groups often call upon Salomon to speak to them about the rebuilding of the temple. The Dome of the Rock, he asserts, will be moved to Mecca. The Muslims will be swept off the Mount so that Israel can exert her rightful sovereignty. All this is necessary before the building of the temple can take place. Churches of the Left Behind point of view are fascinated with such rhetoric and will pay well to have such a convincing personality in their midst. While numbers are hard to come by, it would seem that the budget for the Temple Mount Faithful is largely provided by the patronage of Left Behind believers.

What might come as something of a surprise to these avid admirers is the violence that surrounds the work of the Temple Mount Faithful and their leader, Gershon Salomon. In 1990 the Faithful put up posters announcing plans to lay a four-and-a-half-ton cornerstone for the third temple at Sukkot. The rumor of this plan filtered through the Old City and the surrounding countryside, raising great concern among the Palestinians. Laying a foundation stone for the third temple is, after all, tantamount to seizing the sacred precinct. The uneasiness of times may have added to the tension. It was the third year of the intifada, the Palestinian uprising against Israeli rule. Saddam Hussein had conquered Kuwait and was being hailed by some as the new Saladin who would defeat the West. Two things went wrong: the fact that the police had refused permission for the plan went unnoticed by the Palestinians, and the rising apocalyptic feelings among the Palestinians went unnoticed by the Israeli police. While Salomon and the Faithful were elsewhere celebrating a water libation, several thousand Palestinians gathered to protect the Haram. Thinking that Salomon was approaching, the Palestinians began throwing rocks at the twenty thousand Jewish worshipers gathered at the Wall below. The badly outnumbered security force opened up with live fire, killing a score of Palestinians. Riots spread throughout the normally peaceful Arab towns in Israel. In the wake of the violence and loss of life, Salomon had no qualms about the bloodshed or diplomatic damage to Israel. In reflecting on the matter he spoke proudly about how the cornerstone affair brought international attention and a wave of interest in the Christian world in the Temple Mount and his movement.

The shocking approval of violence by Salomon does not seem to have made much of a stir among dispensationalists. It would seem that violence is not a problem as long as someone else is perpetrating the action itself. Since God is sovereign and will bring to pass what is to come, the means by which it is accomplished is up to him. The confluence of ideas surrounding the need to rebuild the temple is enough to make the followers of the Left Behind point of view allies of the radical Temple Mount Faithful irrespective of their views on violence.

Secular Zionists are not the only ones that populate the fertile ground of apocalyptic vision. Gush Emunim was born out of a religious interpretation of the events surrounding the war of 1967. Rabbi Tzvi Yehudah Kook is convinced that the Holy One has given the land to his people through obvious miracles. The beginning of redemption is clearly written in the signs of the times. And while Kook does not set a particular date for the coming of the Messiah, it is certain that current events are a part of the drama of the End—a fact that has put the Gush Emunim at odds with any attempt to make peace in the Middle East.

The main sticking point has to do with the land. According to Kook's theology the state must not give up any territory in an effort to win concessions and the hope of living with Palestinian neighbors. To do so would be to refuse the promise of God in the giving of the land to Israel and to be complicit in thwarting the beginning of redemption provided in the miraculous events surrounding the 1967 War. That is why Kook and his followers hailed the election of the conservative Menachem Begin. They had hoped that he would maintain a hard line. But when he began to talk with Egyptian leader Anwar al-Sadat at Camp David in 1978, offering the entire Sinai for peace with their southern neighbor, shock waves went through the Gush Emunim.

Already by this time the organization had led the way in creating settlements in the newly occupied territory. This was thought to be the most direct way of assuring that newly acquired territory not be used as exchange for promises of peace. By placing Israeli citizens in contested areas, the political configuration of the region was given a default position favoring continued occupation. In their success at doing this the Gush have become the leading force in religious Zionism. Politically they have had allies in the government, but there have also been seasons in which leadership of the country has not seen things their way. The Gush Emunim have stood fast against ceding any land in negotiations with the Palestinians.

Rabbi Kook opposes setting foot on the Temple Mount. Only God's action will bring about the coming of the Messiah. Not all his followers share that same restraint. Menachem Livni, with the aid of several militant members of Gush Emunim, devised a plan to purifiy the Mount. For two years, the conspirators studied the Mount not as a sacred site so much as a target to be demolished. Aerial photos revealed every detail. Twenty-eight specially devised charges were to be placed on the pillars in the Dome. Livni was a careful man who had even calculated which way the Dome would fall. The explosives had been stolen from the Israeli military. But before the event took place, the Israeli police made arrests.

The full extent of the conspiracy only came out after the interrogations began. The conspirators thought they were working for redemption. The judge saw it differently. Destroying the Dome would have unleashed a religious war with hundreds of millions of Muslims, which would have caused the national conflict between Jews and Arabs to pale in comparison.

At his trial Livni was entirely unrepentant. He was convinced that if the government would not purify the Mount it was up to him to do it. He and two others were sentenced to life for involvement in an attack at the Islamic College where three students were murdered and thirty-three were wounded. But they left prison in fewer than seven years through the commutation of their sentences. The expensive legal defense of the militants was more than covered by money sent from American Jews and Left Behind Christians. The Israeli justice system treated them much better than they deserved—almost as though their only fault was an overabundance of patriotism.

Gush Emunim has received funds from conservative Christian groups. In addition, they have been aided in their political stands by several pro-Israel Christian organizations. One such organization is The Christian Friends of Israeli Communities founded in 1995 by Colorado Springs businessman Ted Beckett. It is designed to "support the brave pioneers who have settled in the heartland of biblical Israel."[28] This goal is accomplished by linking settlements with Christian churches and individuals. The idea is to build bridges of understanding between Christians and Jewish settlers. The Adopt-A-Settlement program allows a Christian church to identify with and support one settlement on the Israeli frontier (called by Beckett's group the heartland of biblical Israel). Each congregation sets up a team to make contact with the settlement and handle fundraising, lobbying, and letter writing on behalf of Israel. Solidarity trips and various projects are generated through the connections that rapidly develop. To date, contributors have provided communication equipment, funding for library and clinic facilities, musical instruments for the children of the settlements, emergency equipment, financial and emotional support for refugees, and more. Current projects are listed on the website with their respective price tags. Browsers are encouraged to make contributions to help the people of the settlements.

The organization is based on the belief that the peace process is flawed and has failed. "Christian Friends of the Israeli Communities (CFOIC) was established in 1995 in response to the Oslo process." Israel's Labor Party government stopped funding the settlements in 1993 to spur peace negotiations. Beckett believes this action ran counter to the clear teaching of the Bible. As with many other pro-Israel organizations that are prophecy driven, CFOIC is committed to the belief that the land is given to the nation of Israel exclusively. Any exchange of land for peace is a violation of God's intention for the region. "CFOIC brings unconditional support to the Jewish Communities and partners with the dedicated pioneers of biblical Israel to fulfill biblical prophecy." The political stand taken by CFOIC is consistent with the prophectic views of dispensationalism.

We turn now to a brief description of the Temple Institute, founded by Rabbi Yisrael Ariel. According to their website, the Institute was established in 1987. It is a nonprofit educational and religious organization dedicated to "every aspect of the biblical commandment to build the Holy Temple of G-d on Mt. Moriah in Jerusalem."[29] The short-term goal is to educate and raise awareness for this project by offering seminars, sponsoring research, publications, and conferences that engage and convince the public. In the long term the Institute is committed to action and activism that will bring about the building of the temple in our time.

The major focus of the Institute, up to this time, has been the research and construction of the sacred vessels for service in the Holy Temple. Each item is thoroughly researched so that they are made according to the exact specifications set out in the Bible. Craftsmen have completed musical instruments to be played by the Levitical choir, the golden crown of the High Priest, and gold and silver vessels to be used for incense and sacrificial services. Special mention is made of the completion of the seven-branched candelabra of pure gold, the golden Incense Altar, and the golden Table of the Showbread, which together form the central vessels of the Divine Service.

The work of preparing the items necessary for temple worship has not gone unnoticed. Having the replicas at the ready for the time when the temple will be built increases the anticipation of what these individuals assume will happen without doubt. Tim LaHaye mentions this work approvingly, not by name but as proof that we are very near the time of fulfillment. What he does not mention are the overt actions undertaken by this group to force the building of the temple.

In March of 1983 Yisrael Ariel and thirty-eight of his yeshiva students set out on their way to the Temple Mount. Plans included tunneling under a portion of it and then offering up Passover prayers. They may have been under the conviction that if they held some claim to the Mount, however tenuous, it would have forced the issue with the Muslim administrators and the Jewish public. Their plans were foiled by the police, who turned them back before they reached their goal. In 1989 Ariel and Joel Lerner, the Director of the Sanhedrin Institute, gained entrance to the Temple Mount. They had decided to offer a Passover sacrifice, the first since the destruction of the temple in AD 70. They hoped this action would clear the way for the reclamation of the holy precinct and accelerate plans for the building of the temple. Standing behind these actions is the conviction that heavenly plans—which include a third temple—can be aided by earthly deeds. To state it in other words, decisive human action can force God to respond.[30]

Ariel approves of violence to meet his own ends. During the mid- and late-1980s, as a prominent leader of the Tzfiyah (Expectation) ideological circle, he provided support and wrote approvingly of the jailed members of the Jewish underground. While others in the organization were satisfied to say that all of Israel's problems—from war to hyperinflation—were divine punishment for not rebuilding the temple after 1967, Ariel went much farther. He asserted that the commandment "Thou shalt not murder" applies only to killing a Jew. Killing a non-Jew, in his radical interpretation, is a different kind of sin that ought not be adjudicated by human courts but should be left up to God alone. Ariel's position is highly critical of any religious Jew who hesitates to take decisive action to rebuild the temple. It is his view that all Christians and Muslims are idolators and that Judaism, when rightly understood, forbids allowing them to dwell in the Land of Israel.[31]

Ariel's virulent and violent views have not kept Christians of the Left Behind point of view from flocking to his Institute. It is said that over one hundred thousand visitors a year tour the Institute with its video productions and displays of newly crafted implements ready for use in the yet-to-be-built temple. The Institute has made a point of attracting Orthodox yeshiva students for educational purposes, but the greater proportion of visitors are not Jewish. Dispensational tour groups to Israel have made the Institute a regular stop on their itineraries. In fact it has been suggested that if evangelical Christians did not give their support, a large portion of the Temple Institute's funding would dry up and would be much more difficult for them to operate.

This is not likely to happen in the short term, because dispensational Christians view the work of the Temple Institute as fulfilling prophecy. The issue is made more problematic by the way in which the "facts" are presented. In reading the popular authors of the Left Behind point of view, one is given the impression that the Jewish people as a whole are looking to rebuild the temple. This is not the case. Some Orthodox Jews do believe that the third temple will be built, but that it will happen in the time of the Messiah; human hands cannot bring it about. Conservative and Reformed Jews are not looking for a new temple, and synagogue worship has replaced the bloody sacrifices. Return to the older form of worship is not anticipated. The nonreligious of Israel clearly have no interest in rebuilding the temple. So, it would seem that the positions of Ariel and the Temple Institute, Salomon, and the Temple Mount

Faithful, and Kook and the Gush Emunim, are on the extreme political edge of Israeli society.

Left Behind Christians have made alliances with some of the most radical political organizations in Israel based on a dispensational view of prophecy. These alliances and the point of view that produced them have ethical consequences. In closing this chapter I mention just three in order to raise a few questions for consideration.

First, approval and support of these groups condones violence to fulfill prophecy. This must be a sobering word for anyone seriously seeking to be a follower of Christ. Is it enough to respond by saying that it is not *we* who are perpetrating the acts of violence, but that the violence is pursued by one who is a mere instrument in the hands of God to bring about his will? Is it allowable for Christian organizations and individual Christians who know about the views and actions we have discussed to wink and turn away? Clearly there is an argument to be made for the sovereignty of God, who can and does use a number of means to achieve the divine will. Cyrus was the means of expressing divine wrath (Isa 40), but what is a Christian to make of someone like Ariel who states quite openly that the killing of a non-Jew is a sin of a different sort? Doesn't this position violate the very heart of biblical tradition in both its legal structure as well as its wisdom tradition? Is it allowable for a Christian to condone and thus support such a position?

Second, the inflexible prophetic calendar of the Left Behind point of view locks a good portion of the Christian world into one method of dealing with conflict in the Middle East. The Temple Mount becomes the object of prophetic desire and the tension only increases. Prophecy teachers from the comfort of their suburban American homes can happily predict the day when the Dome of the Rock is destroyed, never mentioning the fact that such a move may well be the prelude to another world war. Or if they do, they see that too as a part of God's plan and the good news there, according to dispensational teaching, is that believers will be spared going through the great tribulation. Thus insulated against harm, the rigid prophetic calendar precludes the need for responsible

Christian action that might lead to a concerted effort to negotiate peace and to deal with one's neighbor honestly and openly. As we have seen, land for dispensationalists is off the table as a bargaining tool. Any division of the land is seen as going against God's will and biblical prophecy. For the Left Behind point of view, land cannot be used for an incentive to make the parties sit down face to face. The inflexible calendar has a way of breeding a certain kind of fatalism that makes it unnecessary to move beyond a religious adolescence to full Christian maturity.

Third, The Left Behind point of view leaves us vulnerable to that handful of individuals who conclude that now is the time to clear the ground—to force God's hand and bring about the end of days. The Temple Mount is one of the most explosive pieces of real estate on the planet. Dispensationalists have invested a huge meaning to that land and the dream of rebuilding the temple. We have followed to some small degree the millennial mindset that considers this project to be inevitable. Prophecy teachers will continue to look forward to and promote the violent actions that will trigger the prophetic calendar of events as they understand them. This, unfortunately, seems inevitable. But as we come to the end of this consideration of ethical consequences of the Left Behind series, it is our hope that clearer thinking will win the day and the millennial mindset that has brought the world to the brink so many times before will recede so that a healthier account of God's action in the world will take its place.

Recapturing
the Christian Imagination

It is reported that Albert Einstein said, "I know not with what weapons World War III will be fought, but World War IV will be fought with sticks and stones."[1] This statement of reflection upon the volatility and danger of the nuclear age expresses the considerable ambiguity, disquiet, and fear of the human race as it looks out upon the unknown future. Peering into the future has always been an unsettling project, but even more so now that the world has an explosive factor made exponentially larger through modern technology. The danger factor has been made deeper due to the conflicting interests of people groups and adversarial religious claims.

Science Fiction, more than most other genres, has explored these fears and uncertainties and in the process produced some compelling literature. In 1826 Mary Shelley, the creator of Frankenstein, wrote a novel entitled *The Last Man* in which a devastating disease originating in Turkey sweeps the earth in the year 2073. The end of the world becomes the interpretive backdrop for Shelly's reflections on the turbulent world in which she finds herself. Other novels such as Jack London's *The Scarlet Plague* (1915) use the same device to return humanity to savagery and to ponder the nature of human existence.

The rise of Darwinism in the late nineteenth century resulted in an increase in agnosticism and a turning away from religiously conceived views of the end. In this climate the secular vision of the end does not take up the matter of the wrath of God so much as the utter annihilation of the human race through various means. It could be a comet on collision course with the earth as in Camille Flammarion's *La Fin du monde* (1893–94) which has recently been reissued under the title *Omega: the Last Days of the Earth*. Or, it may be clouds of poison gas cleverly depicted in Sir Arthur Conan Doyle's *Poison Belt* (1915). H. G. Wells mesmerized his audience with a secular version of the apocalypse that features invaders from outer-space. *The War of the Worlds* (1898) has found an enduring place in the cultural imagination through its powerful radio presentation in 1938 with Orson Welles at the microphone and once again with its recent remake as a Steven Spielberg film starring Tom Cruise (2005).

Since the Second World War, fascination with nuclear holocaust and imagery of Armageddon has been widespread. In his book *Millennium Movies: End of the World Cinema*, Kim Newman documents the variations found among the myriad accounts of the end.[2] One can find end time scenarios filled with imaginative mutants and monsters. On the other hand, there are scenes of utter desolation in which humanity is reduced to marauding bands along the lines of Mad Max. One of the recurring themes is that of the common people who are powerless to affect one way or the other the course of world events decided by politicians and generals who never have to give account of their actions.

What is the upside to all these end time scenarios? On the one hand, they simplify conflict in a world that has become too complex to be sanely borne by the average resident of planet Earth. On the other, looking into the abyss of the destruction of the world makes everyday troubles seem insignificant by comparison. The oppressive weight of seeing the world going to pieces and featuring so many nihilistic expressions is made slightly easier to handle if the end offers a new opportunity for humankind or, at the very least, the most hateful elements of everyday existence are done away with.

When seen from a particular vantage point, the Left Behind point of view is of a piece with the versions of the end we have just been discussing. If it can be asserted that culture in general is in the grips of a millennial fever, how much more is that true of the dispensational world of interest? It should be pointed out that dispensationalism developed, as did Darwinism, during the nineteenth century and participates in some of the characteristics that mark that age. If the secular versions of the end attempted to validate their vision on the basis of a scientific rendering of all things, Darby's approach to biblical prophecy, and Tim LaHaye's after him, is also an attempt to render the matter scientifically, albeit on the basis of the Bible. What this means for LaHaye and dispensationalism is that literary forms must give way to literalistic interpretation, apocalyptic must give way to apocalypticism, and Christian imagination must be subsumed under a very specific calendar of end time events.

In what follows, the Left Behind point of view will be compared with other interpretive approaches to the book of Revelation. What we will find is that emphasis on events of the future are tied to the dispensational belief that biblical prophecy secures the reliability of Scripture. Then, a consideration of the nature of apocalyptic literature will be taken up. What we will find is that the Left Behind point of view reads the book of Revelation quite apart from its genre as apocalyptic literature. And finally, a concluding word will be made for reclaiming the Christian imagination. One place to begin is to allow the book of Revelation to function as a source for the refreshment of Christian imagination.

Interpreting Revelation

If you were to attend a large dispensational church, chances are you would not have run across any other way of looking at the book of Revelation. Dispensational pastors are not known to give opposing viewpoints much time. In fact, in the dispensational way of viewing things, if it is not dispensational it is considered to be "liberal" and tending toward apostasy and thus not worth considering. For this reason there are many among the faithful who think that the dispensational point of view is the only way to understand the biblical record. In spite of the impression that dispensational pastors might give, there are several approaches to the book of Revelation.

Traditionally, there are four major schools of interpretive thought with respect to the book of Revelation: the preterist, the historicist, the futurist, and the idealist. There are subgroups under some of the headings and each approach has its respective strengths and weaknesses, but each in its own way attempts to use the last book of the New Testament in a manner that will be helpful for the church. Robert Mounce in his commentary on the book of Revelation observes that "Almost all expositors of the book may be placed without significant reservations into one of the four categories."[3]

The preterist approach holds that the majority of the prophecies of the book of Revelation occur in the first century. Though the prophecies were in the future as John wrote them down, their fulfillment is now past and has become a part of history. This conviction is the source of the name "preterist," which comes from a Latin term meaning "gone by" or "past." Preterist interpretation seeks to understand John's prophecy in the specific historical realities of the time. The church, threatened by the growing demands of emperor worship, came into a time of oppression and persecution. Those who endured to the end share in the final victory of God over the demonic forces and the evil coercion of the totalitarian state. Preterists are convinced that the persecutions of Emperor Nero (AD 64–68) are the occasion for John's writing. The work was meant to steel the first century church against falling away as well as to prepare Christians for the coming destruction of Jerusalem.

The advantage of this approach is that it takes seriously the admonition found in the opening chapter of the book that indicates its contents deal with "what must soon take place" and its admonition that "the time is near." By not relegating the book to some future time period, the warnings and the encouragement it offers are given immediate seriousness. If the book is to take place at some distant time in the future, it is hard to imagine what possible application it might have had for a Christian population facing the hard realities of persecution. The disadvantage of this approach is that it is hard to see how the final victory is historically realized in Revelation 20–22. It is difficult to believe that John envisioned anything less than a complete victory over Satan, the oppressive forces of power politics, and the bringing in of the eternal reign of God. The preterist approach is weakest in giving answer to the questions that arise on this account.

The historicist approach holds that some of the book of Revelation has been fulfilled and some is yet to be fulfilled in the future. The Apocalypse, in this view, is seen as the progressive and continuous fulfillment of prophecy throughout the ages. From the prophecies of Daniel through to the time of John and beyond, the prophecies of Revelation offer an outline of human and ecclesiastical history and the story of the struggle between good and evil until the end of time. As Mounce puts it, John's prophecies are said "to sketch the history of Western Europe through the various popes, the Protestant Reformation, the French revolution, and individual leaders such as Charlemagne and Mussolini."[4] Historicism asserts that the Bible and the book of Revelation speak to the church in all ages. This allows one to see the book as applying equally to each and every era of the church's history and not merely to first century Christians as with preterism, or to end time scenarios as with futurists.

There are at least two disadvantages to this view. In the first instance one has to wonder if the intention of the Spirit of God was to give a detailed outline of the entirety of church history to that first generation of Christians. Much of the included prophecy would be quite incomprehensible to people living centuries before its fulfillment. Second, while there is some degree of accord among historicists with respect to key elements of the prophetic unfolding and certain rules of interpreting prophecy, there is a wide divergence in the interpretation of specific passages. While historicists of the early nineteenth century made much of the French Revolution in their interpretation, by the very nature of the case the Puritans of the seventeenth century who lived well before the French Revolution read the same texts with a very different outcome.

The idealist approach has sometimes been called the "spiritual" approach, because it interprets the book with reference to the struggle between good and evil generally speaking and without regard to any specific historical setting. The book of Revelation is meant to be read in its significance for its time, for our time, and for all time. The book, in presenting the harsh reality of the evil without and the evil within, is a voice of realism and a call to follow the Lord in the way of contradiction that will pierce the thoughts of the mind even as it heals them with peace. It is a word for the believers of the first century who were called to endure in the face of persecution. It is a word for believers today who doubt the sovereignty of God and are tempted to capitulate in the face of evil. The word of the prophecy is "endure to the end and you will receive the crown of life." The book of Revelation offers a message of assurance, hope, and victory.

The advantage of this approach is that it focuses the reader on enduring redemptive principles and not on special events or the particularity of any one historical circumstance. This allows the book to be applied in an infinite number of circumstances depending on the vantage point of the reader. But this strength can also become a great weakness. In this approach the interpretation of the book takes on the look and the feel of the allegorical explanation of the interpreter. In other words, the book becomes unhinged from the intention of the original author and comes under the thrall of the selective interests of the reader. Further, this view seems to ignore the time-frame indicators of the book. Can we really assume that addressing the seven churches of Asia Minor has no historical significance but is only an indicator of what church life might be like at all times and in all places?

The futurist, or eschatological view places great emphasis on the return of Jesus Christ and the final victory of God over the forces of evil. The view holds that almost all of the book refers to things which are yet to happen. At present we are living in the normal period of history. Only when the end of the world is at hand will the specific events of the Apocalypse transpire in time. In an earlier chapter we have seen how this view developed during the nineteenth century as a reaction to the prevailing optimistic view of progress that would gradually eventuate in a Christianizing of institutions and the postmillennial reign of Christ on the earth. Futurism, in its various forms, contends that the kingdom of God will come about as the direct and cataclysmic intervention of God into history. Rather than an optimistic view of the progress of humanity, futurism is based on the conviction that things will get worse toward the end.

This approach is marked by a great number of subgroups. Historic premillennialists deny the doctrine of the secret rapture of the church, but affirm a literal catching up of the saints in the air while the earth is purified for the millennial reign of Christ. Classic dispensationalists, or what could be dubbed the Left Behind point of view, is separated into pre, mid, and posttribulation rapture positions. And as if the field were not confused enough, there is the very new progressive dispensational point of view that seeks to avoid the excesses of classical dispensationalism.[5] All of this makes the head swim. But in the interpretational tug-of-war, the futurist position has the advantage of taking human sin seriously and emphasizing the freedom of God in directing the affairs of nations and exercising divine sovereignty over the time of the end. The disadvantages, especially of the Left Behind point of view, should already be apparent.

Robert Mounce has a conciliatory word to speak in his review of the four major approaches to the book of Revelation. He says that "it is readily apparent that each approach has something to contribute to a full understanding of Revelation and that no single approach is sufficient in itself."[6] With the preterist it must be seen that Revelation speaks about real historical events in symbolic terms. The manner in which language functions here is not as a coded message to tell of Russian helicopters, the European Common Market, and other fanciful notions, but is firmly grounded in the historical circumstances of John's time. With historicists we need to see that Revelation speaks of the one who is worthy to give meaning to all of history. With the futurists we need to affirm the literal overcoming of evil and the establishment of God's kingdom and his rule over all nations. With the idealist we must agree that the book also reveals the principles of God's activity in the world, often in hidden form, and the validity of the message of endurance and hope contained in the book.

Seen in this light, it is no surprise that Mounce can go on to say of the book of Revelation that "The author himself could without compromise be preterist, idealist, historicist and futurist."[7] The breadth of vision embraced in the book of Revelation cannot be contained within the bounds of any one of the interpretive schools of thought. Mounce is simply bringing to voice the seriousness with which a new generation of scholars is taking the complex character of Revelation. That is why many of the newest commentaries defy simple categorization in the older interpretive camps. The highly respected G. B. Caird, for example, claims that whatever earthly realities John is pointing to in the symbolism of the book will be accomplished "quickly _in their entirety._"[8] Caird is convinced that John's prophecy has the immanent persecution of the church in view, not the end, the final crisis of world history, the emergence of the Antichrist and the coming of Jesus in victory and judgment. It might seem that this approach to the book would place Caird in the preterist camp. But this would not do justice to the fact that Caird, even though he asserts that the force of John's prophecy is to apprise believers of the nature of their suffering, does not foreclose on the glimpses that the apocalypse gives to those larger realities that lie out beyond the imminent danger of persecution.

Caird's approach is driven by a concern to do justice to the vitality and the complexity of the language of the apocalypse. Readers of the book of Revelation must take into account the conventions that apply to it as apocalyptic literature. Just as poetry is not read as though it were history, in the same way, justice cannot be done to Revelation if it is read as though it were just a highly symbolic gospel account. The language of John is framed in such a manner that the connections of heaven and earth, endemic evil and God's overcoming righteousness can be conveyed to the readers on several levels simultaneously. John's apocalypse brings together vision, theology, and artistry in a sophisticated and powerful synthesis. As Caird puts it, "Much of the New Testament is written for those who have ears to hear, but this book is written for those who have eyes to see; and for a generation whose mental eye has been starved of imagery, it is in some ways the most important book in the New Testament."[9] Whether one agrees with the specifics of Caird's interpretation or not, shifts are taking place in the reading of Revelation that challenge some of the older ways of embracing the book.

Apocalyptic or Apocalypticism?

The manner in which we read the last book of the Bible will depend largely on what kind of book we think it to be. The meaning we hope to find in it will be fixed by the kind of literature it is and the conventions appropriate to its genre. The approach with which we use to hear and "see" its claims on us as participants in the divine story determine in large measure how it functions in our worship and teaching.

Richard Bauckham points out that the book of Revelation belongs to three literary forms: letter, prophecy, and apocalyptic. In the first instance Revelation is a letter addressed to seven churches in first century Asia Minor. The conventional forms of letter writing appear early on with the greeting, "Grace to you and peace from him who is and who was and who is to come . . ." as well as at the conclusion of the work (22:21). The circumstances of these congregations are the historically specific context into which John must speak. Revelation is also prophecy intended to be read aloud in worship. As we are told, "Blessed is he who reads aloud the words of the prophecy, and blessed are those who hear, and who keep what is written therein, for the time is near" (1:3).

The book of Revelation is also a revelation or an *apocalypse*. The term "apocalypse" comes from the Greek meaning "reveal, or disclose."

The apocalyptic worlds of the Bible in both Old and New Testaments peer beyond the mundane social and political circumstances to reveal the relationship between the divine order and our own. In the case of John, his vision is one that discloses Jesus Christ to those who find themselves in tribulation. The message of endurance in the face of hardship in the present hour is given greater force by virtue of the vision of the final vindication of God at the end of time. "Thus Revelation seems to be an apocalyptic prophecy in the form of a circular letter to seven churches in the Roman province of Asia."[10]

John's work as seer is to communicate a transcendent perspective on this world. The prophecy addresses its hearers in their concrete historical situation—that of Christians in the Roman province of Asia during the first century—giving a clear word as to how to analyze the circumstance by cutting through the ambiguity to the real issues facing the community of faith. Whether persecution, deception, idolatry, or weariness are in view, the prophecy is meant to order the recipients of the letter so that an appropriate response might be made in light of divine command. The ambiguity of the mundane is clarified when put in relation to the events as seen from a heavenly vantage.

The revelation of this heavenly point of view is accomplished in dramatic fashion as John is called in the Spirit into the throne room of heaven. As through an open door the visions of the remainder of the book are viewed and inform the hearers of the prophecy. John is given a glimpse behind history, as it were, so that he can see what is really going on in the events of his time and place. Additionally, he is transported into the future to see what shall take place at the end of the world, so that he can see the present in light of the final victory of God on the last day. The revelation of Jesus Christ brings into focus the ultimate meaning of history and the role that the believers to whom the letter is addressed play. As Richard Bauckham notes, "It is not that the here-and-now are left behind in an escape into heaven or the eschatological future, but that the here-and-now look quite different when they are opened to transcendence."[11]

The book of Revelation makes multiple disclosures. To the historical situation, John's message functions to limit the power of the Roman imperial view of the world, which was the dominant ideology of the day. The power oppressive politics of the time, which tended to squeeze everyone into a particular mold, was opposed by the prophetic word given through John's apocalypse. To the difficult and ambiguous question of how one lives a life of faith in the midst of a society that is oblivious or opposed to the righteousness of God, the work gives words of encouragement by which the believers are to overcome. To those experiencing persecution, or those tempted to lose heart in the face of the fact that the evil prosper and the righteous suffer, the book speaks to the question of who is Lord over the world. The Roman Empire that arrogates power unto itself seems to have no rival. But the message of Revelation is that despite appearances, it is God alone who rules his creation and a designated time is coming soon when the old evil empires will be thrown down and his kingdom will be made fully manifest.

This all-too-brief description of apocalyptic literature is some small indicator of the complexity and sophistication of the last book of the New Testament. Any attempt to appropriate its meaning apart from a serious consideration of the conventions by which it must be read is subject to all kinds of misinterpretation. Revelation offers a profound theocentric vision of the coming of God's kingdom. It calls on Christians to confront the idolatries of the first century time period and to participate in the gracious gathering of people of all nations into the family of God. When the reading of this prophecy is fully grounded in the historical context of the seven churches, it is seen to transcend that context and to speak to the contemporary church.

The powerful word that comes to the church in the book of Revelation has not always been allowed to revitalize the church, for there are many ways in which the message can be deflected. Stephen L. Cook outlines a few of those ways in his book *The Apocalyptic Literature*.[12] He claims that interpreters, eager to get a handle on the text and to bring a level of control and comfort into the interpretational task, quickly move to domesticate the apocalyptic literature. Once robbed of their ability to speak on their own terms, the texts are effectively taken as a form of literature that they are not.

Sometimes the domestication comes through spiritual and symbolic readings. Failing to grasp the radical cosmic expectations embedded in apocalyptic texts can cause some interpreters embarrassment, leading them to downplay that aspect of the message. Sometimes the domestication comes about through overly credulous or overly suspicious readings of the text. An interpreter is overly credulous when Revelation is seen as a book of pristine dogma to be read in a purely didactic manner. Interpreters are overly suspicious when, distracted and offended by violence and human limitations found in apocalyptic texts, they lose sight of their beauty, theological richness, and awe.

Cook's analysis also deals with domesticating apocalyptic texts through futuristic readings or through historicized readings. These tendencies can be found among liberal as well as conservative theologians. Apparently domesticating apocalyptic texts is an equal opportunity enterprise! Liberal interpreters tend to rationalize the text saying that the events of Revelation are now behind us as ancient history. This effectively cuts off the biting edge of apocalyptic oriented toward the final vindication at the end of time. This interpretive move may well make the book of Revelation more palatable in an age dubious of the supernatural, but it does so at a price. Conservative interpreters usually take the opposite tack, grounding the message of Revelation in the future so completely that it is hard to know what meaning it might have had for first-century readers. But just as we do a disservice to Revelation if we limit its meaning to a discreet past, so we equally domesticate it by pushing its meaning exclusively into the future.

Revelation is a book that is quite often read as a coded document. The puzzling symbols used in its writing are meant to hide the meaning from the public at large, yielding up its secrets only to the initiated. If the Bible's apocalyptic texts are merely coded documents, then the key to understanding the text is to break the code.

This is done through deciphering the meaning of the given symbols identifying the individuals, nations, and time line indicated. This is the approach taken by the Left Behind series.

Take for example LaHaye's reading of Revelation 18. The opening words of the passage read in the following manner,

> Fallen, fallen is Babylon the great!
> It has become a dwelling place of demons,
> a haunt for every foul spirit, a haunt for every foul bird;
> for all nations have drunk the wine of her impure passion,
> and the kings of the earth have committed fornication with her,
> and the merchants of the earth have grown rich with the wealth of
>   her wantonness." (Rev 18:2b-3)

For LaHaye the meaning can only refer to a literal destruction of the city of Babylon. While he does recognize that not all readers of the text see it that way, he goes on to assert, "Bible prophecy requires the literal rebuilding of Babylon."[13]

This reading of the text fails to recognize the fact that apocalyptic literature quite regularly uses vivid metaphors which enable the writer to speak of the significance of God's dimension of reality while using language tied to events of space and time. "The stars of the heavens and their constellations will not give their light" wrote Isaiah, "the sun will be dark at its rising, and the moon will not shed its light" (Isa 13:10). This is the language that the prophet used as Babylon was being destroyed, never to be rebuilt. To place this kind of event in our own world would be like saying that New York or Los Angeles had just been obliterated. What language would one use to describe such an event and the emotion that it would rightly evoke? That of cosmic destruction, of cataclysmic desolation descended unexpectedly. The point is not that the world has ended; the prophet is using a literary convention to get across his point.

In the case of Revelation 18 there is no mention of stars that will not give their light, but there is mention of the great city. Babylon remains destroyed, and John and his first-century readership are aware of that overriding fact. As such the city has no significance.

But as a symbol of that which is opposed to the kingdom of God it is a useful metaphor in the hands of the prophet. The reference is clearly to more than a mere city. Equally important is the meaning of that city in light of its transgressions. This is the driving force of the text. To put it in the words of N. T. Wright, "[w]hichever city is referred to as 'Babylon' in Revelation 18, the one place it certainly isn't is—Babylon."[14]

The point here is that the Left Behind perspective persists in reading the book of Revelation as a repository of coded information about the events of the end time. This approach to the book does violence to the nature of apocalyptic literature. The conventions for reading apocalyptic are bypassed in favor of placing people, symbols, and events into a rigid time frame. The meaning of the book of Revelation is thus domesticated and distorted in an artificial manner. The end result is that John's apocalypse is transposed from its native vision and art and is subsumed under a nineteenth-century schema produced by J. N. Darby and perpetrated by LaHaye and Jenkins.

The outrageous nature of the misreading can be illustrated by thinking about the conventions of reading poetry. If one were to take the simple poem by William Blake entitled "Lamb" and read it as though it were not poetry, one would make a muddle of the whole enterprise. Or again, if one were to take his poem "The Sick Rose," attempting to decode the work according to a predisposed plan, all the life would go out of this piece of literature which is probably not about a rose at all. Violating the conventions of reading and experiencing apocalyptic literature also yield the same sad results. This is precisely the tragedy of the Left Behind series. In the words of Albert Einstein, "It would be possible to describe everything scientifically, but it would make no sense, it would be without meaning, as if you described a Beethoven symphony as a variation of wave pressure."[15]

Christian Imagination

The tragedy of the Left Behind point of view is that it forecloses on the very purpose and function of the book of Revelation, which is to purge and refresh the Christian imagination.[16] Instead of allowing Christians to see the mundane through the lens of the eternal and how God contests the self-vaunting nature of the power oppressive politics of Rome and consequently all other oppressive regimes, the text is historicized and made to be read in a literalistic manner. In place of the symbolic world into which the believer is invited to enter in order to redirect their response to the world, a rigid end times calendar dictates participation in a prescribed script of prophecy fulfillment developed in the nineteenth century. Preference for reading Revelation as history written in advance has caused Left Behind Christians to discard imagination and to disengage with messy real-life efforts to make things better in the Middle East.

Imagination is an invaluable aspect of vital Christian faith. The case for defending and promoting just such a lively engagement of mind, faith, imagination, and creativity is self-evident. One only needs to call to mind such works as *The Chronicles of Narnia,* or *The Lord of the Rings* in our own time, or *Paradise Lost* and *The Pilgrim's Progress* of an earlier era to be reminded of the value and special function of imagination and the literature in which it is conveyed. Christians have always been nurtured by use of image, storytelling, and settings that invite nuanced participation. Whether the word is spoken by Jesus in a parable or comes by way of an Old Testament prophet, the believing community is drawn into the message through imagination.

A New Testament specialist might make a case for the nonnegotiable role of imagination in the book of Revelation by talking about the nature of apocalyptic literature. And we have already participated to some small degree in that enterprise. But it might be an interesting exercise to make the case for imagination by looking at a famous work from history. A marvelous example of just such a piece of literature that stands at the heart of this kind of creative function is *The Pilgrim's Progress.*

Published in 1678, John Bunyan's work quickly emerged as one of the great English classics. Its success was immediate and complete. A second edition followed almost immediately and its popularity was such that new editions were called for every year. The work was translated into as many languages as the Bible and in 1876 even an edition in shorthand was published! While the vocabulary of the work was the everyday vocabulary of the English working class, its message was one which all strata of society took in with interest and discovery. From commoner to aristocrat, Bunyan's tale of the Christian pilgrim traversing from sin to salvation captured the imagination of the seventeenth-century world and beyond. This outcome could hardly have been in the mind of the author who began this work while in prison.

According to the highly regarded British literary critic Macaulay, at a stroke Bunyan created a masterpiece and the English novel.[17] While others before him had intimated at the form, _The Pilgrim's Progress_ captured within its orbit the essential elements of the emerging genre. While many in our time may read the work for its narrative and dramatic excellence, Bunyan wrote it for the simple biblical truths that it contains. The ethical and the spiritual vision of this simple Puritan thinker were certainly more important to him than were the power of characterization and humor for which the work has rightly become known.

Of the many factors that attract one to _The Pilgrim's Progress_, certainly one is its psychology. Bunyan's straightforward understanding of human nature, and his unblinking commitment to say a thing the way it is, creates an appealing, if sometimes uncomfortable, candor. There is no sugarcoating of human foibles; in fact there is some humor as he sets them out. Bunyan is not a psychologist in a technical sense but his intuitions about people are unnervingly accurate. Bunyan's characters are fundamental types. They lived yesterday, they live today, and they will certainly be with us tomorrow. Without ever having met them we know from experience the likes of Obstinate, Pliability, Worldly Wiseman, Simple, Sloth, Presumption, Formalist, and Hypocrisy.

Another factor that attracts us as readers to Bunyan's dream is the symbolism used. In a great work such as _The Pilgrim's Progress_ it is always the case that more can be suggested than can be fully expressed. Bunyan knows the limitations of language to express a psychic and spiritual experience, so he intimates and suggests. This allows his readers to enter into the story with content of their own, not so as to compete with what he is trying to set out but so that the affective side of the faith experience might have full expression. In this regard Bunyan's dream is not unlike Revelation, which also invites the reader to examine afresh the circumstances of their own travail in the life of the world in order to discern the most faithful path to be taken.

We can also say of Bunyan's work that it has something of an apocalyptic character about it. In the opening lines of the work we find that his is a work of one who dreams; the lines are memorable enough to rehearse.

> As I walked through the wilderness of this world, I lighted on a certain place where was a Den, and I laid me down in *that* place to sleep: And, as I slept, I dreamed a Dream. I dreamed, and behold, *I saw a Man clothed with rags, standing in a certain place, with his face from his own house, a book in his hand, and a great burden upon his back.* [Isa 64:6; Luke 14:33; Ps 38:4; Hab 2:2; Acts 16:30, 31] I looked, and saw him open the Book, and read therein; and, as he read, he wept, and trembled; and, not being able longer to contain, he brake out with a lamentable cry, saying, "What shall I do?" [Acts 2:37][18]

The dream account is reminiscent of John's apocalypse. In it we have record of a world beyond our own, yet with the quality of experience that impinges on our consciousness where we are. In addition, we find his depiction of Christian the pilgrim making his way through dangers that move on the knife-edge of existence, one misstep and all is lost. The trial and tribulation of Christian is like that of the New Testament apocalypse; it is not a matter of endless shades of gray but is conditioned by the most austere of considerations. There are only two colors—black and white—faithfulness or apostasy.

The fundamental question that Bunyan underwrites through the arduous path that Christian takes on his path toward the Celestial City is that of faith. This is a faith that is not a matter of the five or six things one "must" believe to be saved—for this is no faith at all—but is the cruciform path of one who follows the man of the _via dolorosa._

After receiving a word from Interpreter, Christian is directed to an ascending place upon which stood a cross and a sepulcher. As he approached, "his burden loosed from off his shoulders, and fell from off his back, and began to tumble, and so continued to do, till it came to the mouth of the sepulcher, where it fell in." Unexpectedly, the power of the Gospel apprehended him, and Christian found the Father of Jesus Christ making a pronouncement about him. As the account continues,

> Then was Christian glad and lightsome, and said, with a merry heart, "_He hath given me rest by his sorrow, and life by his death._" Then he stood still awhile to look and wonder; for it was very surprising to him, that the sight of the Cross should thus ease him of his Burden. He looked therefore, and looked again, even till the springs that were in his head sent the waters down his cheeks [Zech 12:10]. Now, as he stood looking and weeping, behold three Shining Ones came to him and saluted him with _Peace be unto thee._ So the first said to him, _Thy Sins be forgiven thee_ [Mark 2:5]; the second stript him of his rags, and cloathed him with Change of Raiment [Zech 3:4]; the third also set a mark on his forehead, and gave him a roll with a seal upon it, which he bade him look on as he ran, and that he should give it in at the Celestial Gate [Eph 1:13]. So they went their way.[19]

The pathway of faith is the one upon which Christian receives the absolution, a new garment, and a seal to present on arrival at his destination. He leaves the City of Destruction as a seeker, but once he faces the cross he proceeds as a sinner saved by grace.

The successful completion of Christian's journey toward the Celestial City demands an ever-changing set of responses to the circumstances he faces. Upon entering Vanity Fair, Christian is confronted with the standard of value in a society which is purely economic and commercial. The imposed habits of such a community threaten to squeeze Christian into relinquishing his eternal perspective. But to agree with the unethical position of the inhabitants of Vanity Fair, as tempting as that might be, would be to surrender to a stupid worldly provincialism. Life is more than food and drink and the acquiring of things. Discernment in the moment, or perhaps better, thinking according to the Gospel, is of highest importance to Christian as he proceeds on his journey.

Whether one follows Christian as he enters Vanity Fair, where eternal truths have no market value, or whether one deals with Talkative, who confuses words with ideas, or whether it is upon entering Doubting Castle, where the walls are as thick as one thinks them to be, the silent reader as companion on the journey is called to see the events of everyday life in the light of the eternal. This is very much like the call placed upon the reader of Revelation who is called to view reality in light of the heavenly word come from John the Seer. Particularly sharp in this regard is his critique of Roman power. The representation of Rome as a sea monster and as harlot is a much sharper image than that employed by Bunyan a few centuries later, but in its own way allows the prophet to call into question the conventional wisdom of the day.

In pursuing this line of thinking we are simply asking ourselves the question, "What happens as one enters into the symbolic world of Bunyan's pilgrim?" Or, to state it in another way, "How does imagination function in realizing the goal of this kind of literature?" While quite a lot could be said in answer to the question, I would like to make three suggestions as to how imagination functions in this context. First, the symbolic world or the world of imagination establishes cognitive distance that allows for perspective. Being too close to existence produces a kind of myopia that is hard to discard. Entering into a fresh symbolic world of understanding breaks one out of old patterns of thinking and allows values to change. In this new light one sees matters from a different perspective. Second, the symbolic and sometimes playful interaction leaves room for interpretive power. Dreams do not always make sense when analyzed by waking standards, but often a dream can set into place what hours of analysis fails to reveal. Third, the invitation to participate links the human intellect with human affection. Neither *The Pilgrim's Progress* nor the book of Revelation seeks to impart mere information; theirs is the quite different task of analyzing from divine perspective so as to equip the believer for responsible action in the world. In the case of Revelation it is the call to overcome through the lamb; in the case of *The Pilgrim's Progress* it is to live by the grace of Jesus Christ.

C. S. Lewis, in thinking about how imagination works in fairy tales and fantasy literature, put the whole matter in terms of longing. He says that if we compare fairy tales for children and so-called realistic stories designated for schoolboys or for schoolgirls there is a decided difference. This is how he puts it:

> There is no doubt that both arouse, and imaginatively satisfy, wishes. We long to go through the looking glass, to reach fairy land. We also long to be the immensely popular and successful schoolboy or schoolgirl, or the lucky boy or girl who discovers the spy's plot or rides the horse that none of the cowboys can manage. But the two longings are very different. The second, especially when directed on something so close as school life, is ravenous and deadly serious. Its fulfillment on the level of imagination is in very truth compensatory: we run to it from the disappointments and humiliations of the real world: it sends us back to the real world undivinely discontented. For it is all flattery to the ego. The pleasure consists in picturing oneself the object of admiration.[20]

The boy who reads the school story ends up unhappy, because he cannot have the kind of exceptional success of the story.

The other kind of longing, that for fairy land, is very different. The boy reading such a story does not long for the particulars of the story. There is no desire for there to be dragons in contemporary England, or for the dangers or discomforts of a fairy tale. But the fairy tale has a way of arousing a longing for he knows not what. "It stirs and troubles him (to his life-long enrichment) with the dim sense of something beyond his reach and, far from dulling or emptying the actual world, gives it a new dimension of depth. He does not despise real woods because he has read of enchanted woods: the reading makes all real woods a little enchanted. This is a special kind of longing."[21] It is this special kind of longing that Lewis sees as transforming and the genius of fantasy literature.

More profoundly, Lewis remarks in another place in his writings, that if one finds within one's self a longing that no experience in this life can satisfy, the most reasonable explanation is that it indicates that one was created for another world.[22] Imagination, when taken in the sense that Lewis means it, is a facet of hope, one of the highest of Christian virtues. Imagination that grasps hope does not have a self-reflexive function but drives beyond itself toward the truth.

The book of Revelation invites and produces creative and imaginative engagement. The rich visual world set out in its pages makes room for the kind of eternal longing which Lewis is talking about. Unlike mere sentimentalism, the longing produced by John does not look away from the wrath of God and his judgment. For all things to be put to rights demands the sweeping away of all that stands in opposition to the righteous rule of God. The radical divine "no" is necessary for there to be room for the eternal "yes" of God's full acceptance. Spiritual longing is content to let God be God. Only then can the picture of the new heavens and the new earth pierce the heart with its full sweetness. As the revelator puts it, "and I heard a great voice from the throne saying, "Behold the dwelling of God is with men. He will dwell with them and they will be his people. . . . He will wipe away every tear from their eyes, and death shall be no more, neither shall there be mourning nor crying nor pain any more, for the former things have passed away" (Rev 21:3-4).

The task that stands before the church today and in every generation is to hear once again the words of the prophecy. And when we have entered into the symbolic world of John the seer I think we will find that Lewis was right when he said, "There are two kinds of longing. The one is . . . a spiritual exercise, and the other is a disease."[23]

A Concluding Word

Anticipating the end of the world is a human preoccupation that has both religious and nonreligious forms. We have seen that dispensationalism, or what we have called the Left Behind point of view, is a millennial mindset that has a particular shape because of the nineteenth-century debates out of which it emerged. During the early portion of the twentieth century it grew, keeping pace through the violent passage of two world wars. Through the latter portion of the century it became mainstreamed through the writings of various authors. Now, with the great success of the Left Behind series, we find that in the twenty-first century this form of millennialism has not gone away but has gained adherents.

Coping with a desperate and dangerous world is something we must all do. Reckoning with the realities of an earth marked by genocide, terrorism, injustice of every kind, and change on the scale of *Future Shock* is not for the fainthearted! From this perspective alone one can understand how millennialism with its persistent pessimism of the present and belief in the proximate end of the world as we know it could gain a hearing. But as we also have seen, the Left Behind point of view is an approach to biblical realities. Understanding both sides of the phenomenon is quite important. What we have seen is that the theological positions are not without their social sources and that the social factors within the movement have been given theological justifications.

In what remains it falls to us to ask again, "What price does one have to pay in order to maintain this particular form of Christian millennialism?" "What methods must be employed to make this approach to the world and to the Bible work?" And, "What kind of agenda is dictated by the Left Behind commitments?" These are some of the questions that have been raised and addressed in the prior pages but need to be drawn together at the close of this study.

When I say that the Left Behind point of view is a self-contained system, I mean that it has all the components of a particular language game. It is a proposal for viewing the world and the biblical text in a comprehensive way. It is a world to inhabit, it is a language to be spoken, and it is a worldview to be promoted. To view the Left Behind point of view in this all-encompassing manner may be helpful in highlighting its character as a socially regulated discourse of speech with its own rules and forms of self-understanding.

We have seen that the Left Behind series establishes its own thought world. In this world prophecy is primary. It is the most important single aspect of Scripture, for on the one hand it establishes the reliability and the authority of the biblical text, and on the other it provides the context in which all of life is framed. Prophecy, when understood as history written in advance, then raises the question of significance against the backdrop of world events that are ushering in the end. The only way to properly interpret current events is to have access to the divinely predetermined blueprint for the future. The end time calendar with its built in ambiguity factor allows the true believer to be in possession of insider information regarding what is "really" going on behind the events of the day. The prophecy preacher in this scenario becomes equivalent to the scientific researcher dressed in a white lab coat. There is no reason to question his authority or his veracity on these issues.

But while it may be possible to inhabit this thought world, it is not without its subtle danger. Tuning one's ear to the millennial pitch allows one to hear what no one else does, but it means that a very particular understanding of the world has been purchased. There is no going back to understanding the world as others do. One may gain the society of the initiated, but does it mean that the world is understood more thoroughly or only as one might wish it to be? A dog whistle may gather a few hounds of a particular kind, but it is not an effective instrument for the symphony.

To speak more plainly, the millennial mindset pushes individuals to an extreme edge of Christianity. The price one has to pay for this form of Christian millennialism is very high indeed. As we have seen, one is forced to throw over the witness of centuries of Christian thinkers and teachers to embrace the eccentric views begun by J. N. Darby. It means distancing oneself from the apostolic tradition in exchange for the populist and antiestablishment reading of LaHaye and Jenkins. It means having to embrace the doctrine of the secret rapture of the church over against the clear reading of the text. It means embracing dualisms of several sorts that are opposed to historic Christianity. In short, it means accepting a view of the world seen through a fantastically distorted lens, something like a carnival mirror. Only in this instance, it is not a case of harmless entertainment.

But if the Left Behind point of view is a world to inhabit, it is also a language to be spoken. In fact, it is a language of urgency that increases the anticipation of end times events. This, of course, is the very nature of millennial belief patterns. When LaHaye says that "This generation is closer to the fulfillment of prophecy than any other," he is simply turning up the heat under an already boiling pot. Other verbal cues in this language game include such utterances as, "I only believe what the Bible says." This is code for the Left Behind's commitment to what they call the "literal" interpretation of Scripture. But what it really means is that the one who utters this statement sees things through the lens of this particular form of Christian millennialism. As we have seen, the Bible does not teach a snatching away of the church in the manner in which LaHaye and Jenkins set out in their highly successful series. This millennial reading of the text may be literalistic, but it is not at all a literal reading of the text. Further, we have seen that the language of this form of Christian millennialism is ready to give meaning to random events on the world stage. Whether it is a hurricane, tsunami, or a political action in the Middle East, it may well be tagged as a sign the end is near. When Pat Robertson, John Hagee, or someone else from the Left Behind point of view claim that hurricane Katrina or some other event is a sign of the imminent return of the Lord, the greater portion of American culture is puzzled. This language may be offensive to most, but it is a badge of one's belonging for the insider.

But while it may be possible to speak this language it is not without its subtle dangers. The subtle danger of the language game being played here is that it sequesters itself within its own boundaries. It has its own set of rules that mark it off from the mainstream. Communication with others becomes blurred or even impossible. The language of tradition is always construed as negative. Millennialism of this form, by its very nature, functions within an element of separation. While the separation is from tradition, it applies to Scripture as well. The way that Left Behind obtains the desired separation from so-called apostate forms of Christianity has to do with the method of applying scriptural truth. The text in its historical setting is no longer what is important; the interface with current events is what is valued. A millennial approach to the Bible values this kind of reading. The text is thus read in a highly stylized manner, but unfortunately it makes a muddle of Scripture.

The Left Behind point of view is also a worldview to promote. For the insider, the consequence of viewing the world in this way leads to specific actions. As we have seen, one of the essential elements of this particular form of Christian millennialism is its belief that Israel plays a nonnegotiable role in biblical prophecy. As a result, proponents of this view are engaged in supporting agencies and ministries that promote and fulfill a particular millennial vision. Supporting the nation of Israel at every turn is consonant with the Left Behind end time calendar. In addition, commitment is unswerving for the rebuilding of the temple. This has led to connections with some of the most aggressive politics of confrontation possible. If much of the support is oblique, it still does not sweep away the questions of complicity and culpability.

One of the subtle dangers of the Left Behind point of view is that it dictates a particular form of foreign policy. This allows the millennial believer to bypass the necessity of hard thinking and creative reflection on the problems that plague the Middle East. That is wasted effort if events are already written out in advance. This means that there is no room for option, no value given to peacemaking, and no need for negotiation. In fact the only option held open seems to be praying for the coming conflagration. The appearance of _schadenfreude_ (taking delight in other people's misfortune) is certainly not far away.

What we find in the wake of this all-encompassing thought world is a form of Christianity that is increasingly narrow. The preoccupation with things millennial restricts the parameters of Christian expression and forces aspects of belief into peculiar forms. It creates a Christian subculture that values issues on the extreme edge of Christianity. By striking this kind of profile, central tenants of the Christian message are given less room for consideration. Time is transferred to the pressing matter of reading the signs of the times. All this is to everyone's loss.

No doubt it is well meant and completely sincere. Adherents to the Left Behind point of view are committed Christians looking for the soon return of the Lord. They are convinced of the reliability of Scripture and the saving power of the atoning work of Jesus Christ. But instead of opening out on a freedom that flows from the Gospel we find another principle at work. The millennial mindset, oriented toward reading Scripture as a codebook for an end times calendar, tends to squeeze reality into an overheated corridor that means loss not gain.

The Left Behind series is all about evangelism. The books were written so that the average reader could access the story line and get swept up in the action. The characters of the series were crafted to be appealing and believable. And Jenkins spent extra time creating scenes depicting personal conversion. He admits that this was not easy. But as Jenkins recounts, approximately three thousand individuals have contacted them through e-mail, letters, and personal conversation indicating that they have come to faith through the novels. Many of these prayed the Sinner's Prayer after Rayford, one of the protagonists in the first book. This is the upside of the Left Behind series. My only regret is that these individuals who have had a life-changing experience with Jesus Christ may have a faith that is shaped by the subtle dangers of a millennial madness.

Notes

Chapter 1, pages 1–24

1. Jim Sonnenberg, "Prophetic profits; Christian publisher's success draws rivals," *Crain's Chicago Business,* June 23, 2003.

2. Ibid.

3. David van Biema et. al., "The Twenty Five Most Influential Evangelicals in America," *Time,* February 7, 2005.

4. The Official Left Behind Series Site, "Kids," http://www.leftbehind.com/channelkids.asp (accessed June 5, 2007).

5. Ibid.

6. The Official Left Behind Series Site, "End Times," http://www.leftbehind.com/channelendtimes.asp (accessed June 5, 2007).

7. The Official Left Behind Series Site, "Live for God," http://www.leftbehind.com/channelliveforgod.asp (accessed June 5, 2007).

8. Gershom Gorenberg, "Intolerance: The Bestseller," review of *Left Behind: A Novel of the Earth's Last Days,* by Tim LaHaye and Jerry Jenkins, *The American Prospect* [online], 13, no. 17 (2002), http://www.prospect.org/print/V13/17gorenberg-g.html (accessed June 5, 2007).

9. Mark Hitchcock and Thomas Ice, *The Truth Behind Left Behind,* intro. by Tim LaHaye (Sisters, OR: Multnomah, 2004).

10. Barbara R. Rossing, *The Rapture Exposed: the Message of Hope in the Book of Revelation* (Boulder, CO: Westview Press, 2004).

11. An account of Jessica's story is excerpted on the Left Behind website as well as in Jerry Jenkins and Tim LaHaye, *These Shall Not Be Left Behind* (Carol Stream, IL: Tyndale House Publishers, 2003).

12. The Official Left Behind Series Site, "Interact," http://www.leftbehind.com/channelinteract.asp (accessed June 5, 2007).

13. Robert Rhodes, "Professor critiques 'Left Behind' books," *Mennonite Weekly Review,* March 4, 2003, 2.

14. Online NewsHour Conversation: Left Behind, PBS, December 20, 2004, http://www.pbs.org/newshour/bb/religion/july-dec04/apocalypse_12-20.html (accessed June 5, 2007).

15. Charles Henderson, "Left Behind: Bad Fiction; Bad Faith," http://www.godweb.org (accessed June 5, 2007) and David Cloud, "Left Behind: Tolerable Entertainment, Intolerable Theology," http://www.wayoflife.org (accessed June 5, 2007).

16. Henderson, "Left Behind: Bad Fiction, Bad Faith."

17. Gorenberg, "Intolerance: The Bestseller."

18. Paul Thigpen, *The Rapture Trap: A Catholic Response to "End Times" Fever* (West Chester, PA: Ascension Press, 2002), 237–44.

19. Carl Olsen, *Will Catholics Be "Left Behind"?: A Catholic Critique of the Rapture and Today's Prophecy Preachers,* (San Francisco: Ignatius Press, 2003), 221.

20. Gary DeMar, *End Times Fiction: A Biblical Consideration of the Left Behind Theology* (Nashville, Thomas Nelson Publishers, 2001).

21. Ann Banks, "Popular Fiction: In a nervous world, a series of apocalyptic thrillers continues to dominate bestseller lists," *Washington Post,* October 17, 2004, 10.

22. Gershom Gorenberg, "Intolerance: The Bestseller."

23. Ibid.

24. Ibid.

25. Ibid.

26. Mark Hitchcock and Thomas Ice, *The Truth Behind Left Behind,* 5.

27. Ibid.

28. Online NewsHour Conversation: Left Behind. PBS. December 20, 2004, http://www.pbs.org/newshour/bb/religion/july-dec04/apocalypse_12-20.html (accessed June 5, 2007).

29. Frontline: Apocalypse! "Apocalypticism Explained: America's Doom Industry" http://www.pbs.org/wgbh/pages/frontline/shows/apocalypse/explanation/doomindustry.html (accessed June 5, 2007).

30. Paul Boyer, *When Time Shall Be No More: Prophecy Belief in Modern American Culture* (Cambridge, MA: Belknap Press, 1992), 46–79.

31. Rod Dreher, "Afraid You'll Be Left Behind?" *National Review Online,* November 18, 2002, http://www.nationalreview.com/dreher/dreher111802.asp (accessed June 5, 2007).

32. Charles Henderson, "Left Behind: Bad Fiction; Bad Faith."

Chapter 2, pages 25–50

1. Norman Cohn, _Cosmos, Chaos and the World to Come: the Ancient Roots of Apocalyptic Faith_ (New Haven, CT and London: Yale University Press, 1993).

2. Estevao Bettencourt, "Millenarianism," _Sacramentum Mundi_ 4 (1969): 43–44.

3. For this passage from Dialogue with Trypho 80, I am indebted to Richard B. Hays, _"Carnis Resurrectionem" Exploring & Proclaiming the Apostles' Creed_, ed. by Roger E. Van Harn (Grand Rapids, MI: Eerdmans, 2004), 264.

4. Charles Hill, _Regnum Caelorum: Patterns of Millennial Thought in Early Christianity_ 2nd ed. (Grand Rapids, MI: Eerdmans, 2004), 11–20.

5. Estimates of the dead range anywhere from fifty thousand to two hundred thousand.

6. Shelton Smith, et. al., _American Christianity: An Historical Interpretation with Representative Documents_, vol. 1 (New York: Scribner, 1960), 101–2.

7. Winthrop S. Hudson, _Religion in America: An Historical Account of the Development of American Religious Life_, 2nd ed. (New York: Scribner's and Sons, 1973), 210.

8. Joshua V. Himes, ed., _Miller's Works Volume I: Views of the Prophecies and Prophetic Chronology, selected from manuscripts of William Miller; with a memoir of his life_ (Boston: Joshua V. Himes, 1842), 9.

9. Ibid., 11.

10. Ibid., 20 (rule no. 4).

11. Ibid., 11–12.

12. Ibid., 12.

13. Ibid., 35.

14. William Kelly, ed., _Collected Writings of J. N. Darby Prophetic Vol. 1_ (London: G. Morrish, 20 Paternoster Square, n.d.), 571.

15. Ibid.

16. Darby, _Collected Works_, XI, 156 as cited in Timothy Weber, _On the Road to Armageddon: How Evangelicals Became Israel's Best Friend_ (Grand Rapids, MI: Baker Academic, 2004), 22.

17. C. Norman Kraus, _Dispensationalism in America: Its Rise and Development_ (Richmond, VA: John Knox Press, 1958), 83.

18. Only two biographies on Scofield exist, one eulogizing him and his life, the other excoriating him as unfit for the Christian ministry. Respectively they are Charles G. Trumball, _The Life and Story of C. I. Scofield_ (New York: Oxford University Press, 1920), and Joseph M. Canfield, _The Incredible Scofield and His Book_ (Vallecito, California: Ross House Books, 1988).

19. Ernest Sandeen, *The Roots of Fundamentalism: British and American Millenarianism, 1800–1930* (Chicago: University of Chicago Press, 1970), 222.

20. Following the success of Scofield's notes are others like the Ryrie Study Bible.

21. Sandeen, *Roots of Fundamentalism,* 222.

22. George Marsden, *Fundamentalism and American Culture: The Shaping of Twentieth Century Evangelicalism 1870–1925* (Oxford: Oxford University Press, 1980), 149.

23. Weber, *On the Road to Armageddon,* 105.

24. Ibid.

25. Wilbur Smith, *The Atomic Bomb and the Word of God* (Chicago: Moody Press, 1945), 55.

26. Ibid., 132.

27. Ibid., 190.

Chapter 3, pages 51–74

1. Tim LaHaye and Jerry B. Jenkins, *Left Behind: A Novel of the Earth's Last Days* (Carol Stream, IL: Tyndale House, 1996), 46–47.

2. Tim LaHaye, *Rapture Under Attack* (Sisters, OR: Multnomah Publishers, 1998), 38.

3. Bad Movie Planet. "Left Behind." http://badmovieplanet.com/duckspeaks/reviews/2004/left-behind/ (accessed December 12, 2006).

4. Mark Hitchcock and Thomas Ice, *The Truth Behind Left Behind: A Biblical View of the End Times* (Sisters, OR: Multnomah Press, 2004), 21.

5. The Official Left Behind Series Site. www.leftbehind.com

6. Tim LaHaye and Jerry Jenkins, *Are We Living In the End Times? Current Events Told in Scripture . . . And What They Mean* (Wheaton, IL: Tyndale House Publishers, 1999), 95–96.

7. Tom Wright, *Paul for Everyone: Galatians and Thessalonians* (London: SPCK, 2002), 123.

8. Jesus had to be protected from an edict directed against male children just as Moses had. Jesus sojourned in Egypt before pursuing the remainder of his ministry just as Moses. Like Moses, who fed his people manna in the wilderness, so Jesus miraculously gave his people sustenance in the feeding of the five thousand. Jesus' Sermon on the Mount reminds us of another lawgiver on another mountain. Jesus says to Nicodemus, "And as Moses lifted up the serpent in the wilderness, so must the Son of man be lifted up, that whoever believes in him may have eternal life" (John 3:14, 15).

9. St. John Chrysostom, Homily VIII on 1 Thessalonians, _A Select Library of Nicene and Post-Nicene Fathers of the Christian Church,_ vol. 13 (Grand Rapids, MI: Eerdmans Publishing, 1956), 356.

10. Tim LaHaye and Jerry B. Jenkins, _Left Behind,_ 210.

11. Ibid., 211.

12. Ibid. 212.

13. Gary DeMar, _End Times Fiction,_ 28–29, citing the _Scofield Reference Bible_ (New York: Oxford University Press, [1909] 1945), 1016 n. 1.

14. N. T. Wright, _What Saint Paul Really Said: Was Paul of Tarsus the Real Founder of Christianity?_ (Grand Rapids, MI: Eerdmans, 1997), 36.

15. For more on this point see, Ben Witherington, _The Problem with Evangelical Theology: Testing the Exegetical Foundations of Calvinism, Dispensationalism and Wesleyanism_ (Waco, TX: Baylor University Press, 2005), 93–170.

16. Tim LaHaye, _Rapture Under Attack_ (Sisters, OR: Multnomah Publishers, 1998), 228.

17. Ibid., 33.

18. Ibid., 36.

19. Ibid., 38.

20. Mark Hitchcock and Thomas Ice, _The Truth Behind Left Behind,_ 20ff.

21. George Eldon Ladd, _The Blessed Hope: A Biblical Study of the Second Advent and the Rapture_ (Grand Rapids, MI: Eerdmans Publishing Company, 1956), 61–70. See also, Ben Witherington, _The Problem with Evangelical Theology,_ 111–31.

Chapter 4, pages 75–98

1. Timothy Weber, _On the Road to Armageddon: How Evangelicals Became Israel's Best Friend_ (Grand Rapids, MI: Baker Academic, 2004), 13.

2. Tim LaHaye and Jerry Jenkins, _Are We Living In the End Times?,_ 45.

3. Ibid., 47.

4. Ibid., 54, citing John Walvoord, _Armageddon, Oil, and the Middle East Crisis,_ (rev. ed.) (Grand Rapids, MI: Zondervan, 1990), 105–6.

5. Ibid, 53–55.

6. According to form, the prophecies are always a bit more convoluted than they at first appear. Further explanation reveals that there will be two "regatherings" of Israel, the first in unbelief, the second, at the end of the tribulation period, in belief. Mark Hitchcock and Thomas Ice, _The Truth Behind Left Behind,_ 56–74.

7. LaHaye and Jenkins, _Are We Living In the End Times?,_ 50. A brief account of the Balfour Declaration and the gradual stirrings that led to nationhood is recounted in the following pages.

8. Ibid., 39.

9. Ibid., 43.

10. Ibid., 57.

11. Ibid., 58–59.

12. Gary DeMar, *End Times Fiction,* 204.

13. LaHaye and Jenkins, *Are We Living In the End Times?,* 59.

14. Gary DeMar, *End Times Fiction: A Biblical Consideration of the Left Behind Theology,* 74–75.

15. Ibid., 91.

16. N. T. Wright, *Jesus and the Victory of God,* vol. 2: Christian Origins and the Question of God (Minneapolis, MN: Fortress Press, 1996), 365.

17. Vern S. Poythress, *Understanding Dispensationalists,* 2nd ed. (Philipsburg, NJ: P & R Publishing, 1987), 58.

18. Tim LaHaye and Jerry Jenkins, *Are We Living in the End Times?,* 77. The larger discussion of the drift toward apostasy extends from 73–78.

19. Poythress, *Understanding Dispensationalists,* 59.

20. Mark Hitchcock and Thomas Ice, *The Truth Behind Left Behind,* 63. The quotation is from Arnold Fruechtenbaum, *Footsteps of the Messiah* (Tustin, CA: Ariel Ministries Press, 1983), 65.

21. For example, J. Alec Motyer, *The Prophecy of Isaiah: an Introduction and Commentary* (Downer's Grove, IL: InterVarsity Press, 1993), 125–26.

Chapter 5, pages 99–127

1. Timothy Weber, *On the Road to Armageddon: How Evangelicals Became Israel's Best Friend,* 45–66.

2. Ibid., 46.

3. Ibid., 47.

4. Tim LaHaye and Jerry Jenkins, *Are We Living in the End Times?,* ix.

5. Ibid., 10.

6. Bernard McGinn, *Visions of the End: Apocalyptic Traditions in the Middle Ages* (New York: Columbia University Press, 1979), 10.

7. Richard Landes, "Millennialism" *Merriam-Webster Encyclopedia of World Religions* (Springfield, MA: Merriam-Webster, 1999), 727–37.

8. Clyde E. Hewitt, *Midnight and Morning* (Charlotte, NC: Venture Books, 1983), 99.

9. Tim LaHaye and Jerry Jenkins, *Are We Living in the End Times?,* 86.

10. See the analyses of Stephen D. O'Leary, *Arguing the Apocalypse: A Theory of Millennial Rhetoric* (Oxford: Oxford University Press, 1994), 154–57, and Gary DeMar, *End Times Fiction,* 6–8.

11. As cited by O'Leary, 157.

12. Tim LaHaye and Jerry Jenkins, _Are We Living in the End Times?_, 92.

13. Ibid., 94.

14. Ibid., 143.

15. Ibid., 140–41.

16. Ibid., 142.

17. Yaakov Ariel, "How Are Jews and Israel Portrayed in the Left Behind Series?" in _Rapture, Revelation, and the End Times: Exploring the Left Behind Series_, ed. Bruce David Forbes and Jeanne Halgher Kilde (New York: Palgrave Macmillan, 2004), 160.

18. David D. Grafton, "The Use of Scripture in the Current Israeli-Palestinian Conflict," _Word & World_ 24 (2004): 32.

19. Grace Halsell, _Forcing God's Hand: Why Millions Pray for a Quick Rapture—and Destruction of Planet Earth_ (Washington, DC: Crossroads International Publishing, 1999), 24.

20. Tim LaHaye and Jerry Jenkins, _Are We Living In the End Times?_, 119.

21. Christians for Israel International. www.c4israel.org (accessed August 5, 2007).

22. Timothy Weber, _On the Road to Armageddon_, 250–51.

23. Temple Mount website, www.templemountfaithful.org (accessed July 26, 2007).

24. Gershom Gorenberg, _The End of Days_, 123–24.

25. Ibid., 139.

26. Ibid., 158.

27. Ibid., 159.

28. Christian Friends of the Israeli Communities are found at http://cfoic.com

29. Temple Institute is found at http://www.templeinstitute.org

30. Randall Price, _The Coming Last Days Temple_ (Eugene, OR: Harvest House Publishers, 1999), 401–2.

31. Gershom Gorenberg, _The End of Days_, 176.

Chapter 6, pages 128–148

1. Albert Einstein quotes, http://www.humboldt1.com/~gralsto/einstein/quotes.html (accessed January 8, 2007).

2. Kim Newman, _Millennium Movies: End of the World Cinema_ (London: Titan Books, 1999).

3. Robert Mounce, _The Book of Revelation_, The International Commentary on the New Testament (Grand Rapids, MI: William B. Eerdmans Publishing Co., 1977), 41.

4. Robert Mounce, *Revelation*, 42.

5. For a brief description of this position see the chapter "Progressive Dispensationalism," in C. Marvin Pate, general editor *Four Views on the Book of Revelation* (Grand Rapids, MI, Zondervan, 1998): 133–175.

6. Robert Mounce, *Revelation,* 43.

7. Ibid., 44.

8. G. B. Caird, *The Revelation of Saint John the Divine,* Harper's New Testament Commentaries (New York: Harper & Row, 1966), 12.

9. Ibid., 13.

10. Richard Bauckham, *The Theology of the Book of Revelation,* New Testament Theology, gen. ed. James D. G. Dunn (Cambridge, UK:Cambridge University Press, 1993), 2.

11. Ibid., 7–8.

12. Stephen L. Cook, *The Apocalyptic Literature,* Interpreting Biblical Texts (Nashville: Abingdon Press, 2003), 39–61.

13. Tim LaHaye, *Revelation Unveiled,* rev. and updated ed. of *Revelation Illustrated and Made Plain* (Grand Rapids, MI: Zondervan, 1999), 279.

14. N. T. Wright, *The Millennium Myth* (Knoxville, TN: John Knox Press, 1999), 30.

15. Einstein quotes. www.humboldt1.com/~gralsto/einstein/quotes.html (accessed January 8, 2007).

16. As Richard Bauckham puts it, "We have suggested tht one of the functions of Revelation was to purge and refurbish the Christian imagination. It tackles people's imaginative response to the world, which is at least as deep and influential as their intellectual convictions." *The Theology of the Book of Revelation,* 159.

17. J. W. Mackail, *The Pilgrim's Progress: A Lecture Delivered At the Royal Institution of Great Britain, March 14, 1924,* (London & New York: Longmans, Green and Co., 1924), 9.

18. John Bunyan, *The Pilgrim's Progress, from this world to that which is to come delivered under the similitude of a dream wherein is discovered the manner of his setting out his dangerous journey and safe arrival at the desired country,* The Christian Library (Uhrichsville, OH: Barbour Books, 1990), 1.

19. Ibid., 36.

20. For more on this topic, see C. S. Lewis, "On Three Ways of Writing for Children," *Of Other Worlds: Essays and Stories* (New York and London: A Harvest/HBJ Book, 1952), 28–30.

21. Ibid.

22. C. S. Lewis, *Mere Christianity* (New York: HarperCollins Books, 2001), 136–37.

23. Ibid.

Name Index

Scripture Index

Subject Index